NO MORE STRANGERS

NO MORE STRANGERS

by Philip Berrigan, S.S.J.

INTRODUCTION BY *Thomas Merton*

The Macmillan Company, New York

To my brother, Father Dan, S.J.,
without whom neither my priesthood
nor this book would be possible.

My lasting gratitude to my brethren in service of the Negro, for their encouragement, advice, and well-founded criticism. In particular, my Superior, the Very Reverend George F. O'Dea, S.S.J.; my censor, the Reverend Joseph L. Waters, S.S.J.; the Reverend Eugene P. McManus, S.S.J.; the Very Reverend Arthur J. O'Leary, S.S.J.

The Author wishes to thank the following for permission to reproduce copyrighted material: Alfred A. Knopf, Inc., for *Resistance, Rebellion and Death,* by Albert Camus; Harper & Row, for *The Perennial Philosophy,* by Aldous Huxley and *The Art of Loving,* by Erich Fromm; Harcourt, Brace & World, Inc., for *Darkwater,* by W.E.B. DuBois, used with the permission of the Estate of W.E.B. DuBois; for *Be Not Afraid,* by Emmanuel Mounier, published by Sheed & Ward Inc., N.Y.; for *Catholicism,* by Henri de Lubac, published by Sheed & Ward, Inc., N.Y. and used with the permission of Burns & Oates Ltd., London; The Publishers Newspaper Syndicate for a quotation from "Is the Negro a Man—or Not?" by Sydney J. Harris, syndicated columnist for the Chicago Daily News.

The Author also wishes to thank the following periodicals for permission to quote copyrighted material: *Jubilee,* for "The Meaning and Constructive Value of Suffering" by Pierre Teilhard de Chardin, which appeared in the June 1962 issue; and *The Catholic World,* for "Pastor Lackmann's Way to Unity" by Eva-Maria Jung, which appeared in the September 1961 issue.

The Author wishes to thank the following for permission to use in somewhat different form the articles: "Racial Patterns and the Christian" which appeared in the October 1964 issue of *New City;* "Race and the Christian Conscience" which appeared in *Continuum;* "Segregation and the Nuclear Arms Race" published in *Crosslight,* Vol. 4, No. 4 (1963); "The Nature of Christian Witness" which appeared in the July-August issue of *Perspectives.*

Contents

Introduction

What is the real meaning of "renewal" and *aggiornamento* in the Church? The terms are familiar enough in these days of the Second Vatican Council. So too are other familiar phrases about "the emerging layman," "lay theology," "the Church and the modern world." What are they all about?

Sometimes it appears that these expressions are used with only the most perfunctory attempt to convey a meaning. They tend to be hopeful incantations. They have become favorite catch phrases indicating a general climate of optimism, an awareness or a pious hope that the Church is not altogether out of date in the space age. Yet this notion of updating tends to be equivocal, through contagion with the ambiguities of a fast-moving technology extrapolated in the processes of a marketing society. In what sense is the Church getting up to date? In the same sense as this year's Ford or Chevrolet?

Obviously Pope John did not mean anything of this sort when he called the Vatican Council. It is true that we do occasionally hear of accommodations that will amount to a considerable shift of scenery; but the updating we look for must surely be something a little more fundamental than a new uniform for the Swiss guards at the Vatican—or even a new habit for sisters at the parochial school.

A great deal of the loud optimism about renewal and *aggiornamento* appears to come from people who are working hard to allay deep anxieties about themselves, the Church and even the Catholic faith. These are the ones (and they form a majority) who are not yet used to associating anguish with the life of faith. For these it is axiomatic, and always has been, that the life of faith brings total security and an absolute lack of questioning or of uncertainty in any point whatever. Yet even they are bound to take account of the fact that unbelievers set very little store by their security and seem determined to get along without it. It has until recently been customary to dismiss this evident hardness of heart as a sign of reprobation. But now it becomes necessary, or so it would seem, for the Christian to break through to these hard hearts and establish some basis of communication. The Church now has to be heard speaking their language and sharing some of their concerns. Not only that, she must convince them that she is just as modern as they are, just as concerned with efficiency and up-to-date methods, just as alert, just as smart, just as impatient of antique formality. For these Christians there seems to be a great need of recognition, of an assurance, on the part of the modern world, that their existence is still relevant. They desire not only to pray silently and defiantly for the world; they also want the world to admit that it *needs* them. And this is a tall order.

The Vatican Council has indeed been getting an extraordinarily good press in the secular media, and the efforts made by the Council to update the Church are regarded as news even for non-Christians. Yet experience shows that readers of the press and viewers of TV tend to accept without protest the judgment of the press and TV as to what constitutes news. Does this docile acceptance imply real interest?

Those who take too superficial a view of *aggiornamento* may tend to draw encouraging conclusions merely from the fact that the old Church can still get such good coverage. This implies acceptance of the delusion that one's real importance can be gauged by the Gallup polls. But this is not renewal of the Church; it is only the renewal of her image, or should we say her myth?

The message of the present book can be summed up as a fervent protest against the idea that all the Church needs is a new "posture," a refurbished image, or an American accent. Father Berrigan is not impressed by the Madison Avenue style in religion. His book is a plea for a much deeper consideration of *aggiornamento* and of the layman's role in the Church's life. It is a forthright denial that Catholics can remain satisfied with a new jargon, a new ideology, a new mystique that will successfully engage the attention of the modern technologist, the man of science, the cold-war politician and—who knows?—even the Marxist. The Church is not going to make her way in the modern world merely by ecclesiastical newspeak and theology in timestyle.

Father Berrigan belongs to the *avant-garde* in liturgy as in other things, but he is not one who will accept the idea of a new ritual and a new liturgical language unless the Christians who participate in the new liturgy recognize the full social implications of their doing so. What is the good of "full active participation" in the Eucharistic Sacrifice if one remains indifferent to the struggle of the Negroes for civil rights, or if one is benign toward Negroes in theory but hostile to them in concrete fact? What is the good of hearing the gospel of peace proclaimed in one's mother tongue if one remains committed to policies based on hatred, fear, suspicion and full readiness to cooperate in genocide? That is why this book contains one of the best Catholic analyses of the race question in the U.S. and another on the arms race in which the author makes the incisive remark that all the great social problems of our time have to be seen as signs of "the unfinished Redemption" and consequently as challenges to Christian faith and Christian concern.

Pope Paul has made some significant, not to say radical, gestures —for instance his symbolic renunciation of the tiara, his pilgrimage to Bombay, there to plead with the world to renounce the suicidal arms race and devote the money instead to helping the desperately poor, who form the majority of the earth's population. But it will be of scant significance to set aside the tiara, the symbol of papal temporal power, and yet still retain the obsolete apparatus of a clerical bureaucracy that frustrates or delays every attempt to liberate the apostolate and the Christian witness from futile institutional routines. The great battle of the Second Vatican Council has been between the forces that seek a real and fundamental renewal that will reshape the whole human organization of the Church and those who, dreading a real change of structures, seek to maintain the forms and routines esatblished to meet the needs of the sixteenth century, while merely giving the Church a twentieth-century façade.

Clearly, then, *aggiornamento* means something more than supplying the old clerical apparatus with humming IBM machines through the courtesy of business and industry (in return for a formal ecclesiastical blessing upon intercontinental ballistic missiles).

To put it very plainly, the thing that is not yet getting through unambiguously either to the clergy or to the laity is that the old institutional clericalism of the Church faces the need for radical change, from the Roman curia on down, via the diocesan curia, right into the parish where Father dictates (or withholds) the final answer on everything from liturgy and marriage problems to questions of social justice and social action which are strictly the business of the laity. Such a reform, of course, implies a much more radical approach to such questions as the priesthood, the religious life, seminaries and the lay apostolate than has as yet been suggested in the Council schemata on these points, though a minority of Bishops and *periti* have already raised the great questions in all their stark urgency. The job of *aggiornamento* in the Church requires not merely that the Council should set in motion new policies to be implemented by the clergy and religious, using zealous lay Catholics as docile instruments. It requires the formation of a new clergy and a new laity, a clergy that will not only have a real empathy and understanding of the problems of the layman and of his world but will even be willing to recognize that the Church belongs to the layman, is *for* the layman and *of* the layman, and is indeed a lay Church. For it is the laity who are the "Chosen People of God" even though the clergy are, it is true, especially chosen and set apart by vocation to give themselves to God and to service of the Church. But the very fact that the clergy is called to *serve* the laity highlights the importance of the laity in the Church.

Renewal of the Church depends on the difficult and sacrificial task of changing a clerical Church back into a lay Church— sacrificial especially for the clergy and religious who will have to participate in their own downgrading, who will need to understand that *they alone do not constitute the Church*, that their holiness is not the beginning and the end of all the Church's strivings, that the worship *they* offer to God is not the main reason for the Church's existence.

Father Berrigan is here following the paths opened up by Congar and Karl Rahner, not to mention Emmanuel Mounier and Teilhard de Chardin. He directs a clearsighted and perhaps in some ways ruthless attack on the myth of a purely clerical Church —a Church in which Christian holiness is priestly and conventual holiness, in which the clergy and the religious keep everything going by their dedicated lives. In such a Church the layman is at best an outsider who makes a desperate effort to live as a religious in the world while serving as an instrument in clerically directed projects. At worst the layman is a mere passenger who hangs onto the Church and manages, by following clerical admonitions, to keep himself from falling off into the abyss of communism and unbelief.

Of course one must face the fact that there are cogent pragmatic reasons why the Church has become so completely clericalized. A trained and disciplined corps of ecclesiastics makes it possible for the institution to be well organized and efficiently run. It is a real power for unity, and there is no question of getting along without such trained and dedicated Christians. There is no doubt that the task of creating a fervent and profoundly enlightened Christian laity demands the indispensable efforts of the clergy themselves. But the clergy must take a totally new attitude toward lay action and lay holiness. They must see that it is not merely a second-rate version of clerical action and clerical holiness. And this new attitude toward the layman and his world is going to prove decisive in the spiritual renewal of the clergy themselves.

To regard the Church as primarily clerical and conventual has dangerous consequences because it produces a radical split between two completely separate realms of "spirituality" and "secularity." The "spiritual" or sacred realm is confined to the convent or the sanctuary, or to the half hour of Mass and Communion and to other moments of duty and devotion in which the layman seeks for the time being to behave like a minor seminarian. The "secular" takes in everything else. Naturally this same split affects the priest and the religious even more deeply than the layman, since the priest and religious are trained to give special regard to certain exercises of piety which presumably save their active work from becoming a debacle but which tend to become more and more perfunctory as active (and secular) concerns absorb more and more of the day, infecting it with a sense of guilt.

The term "lay monasticism" is used disparagingly by Father Berrigan in this connection to indicate an unrealistic spirituality, in which the layman seeks the sacred and godly by turning away from the concrete realities of his own everyday life. Actually, I might mention that in monastic circles the term has quite different connotations and suggests something of the best present tendencies in monastic reform. "Lay monasticism" is a form of monastic life in which the monks ordinarily do not become clerics or priests and in which consequently they have a simpler and less regimented life, a vernacular office, are not subject to the rather arid formalities of seminary education and can therefore be formed more properly and more freely as monks. This represents a return to the original simplicity and spontaneity of the monastic idea in which the monk was in fact *a layman* living apart in poverty, by the work of his hands, either alone or in a likeminded community.

Father Berrigan's book is not concerned with monks, but the point is worth mentioning here because it shows how, at both extremes, there is this same tendency to draw inward toward the center. The layman now begins to realize that he is required only to be himself and not to justify his existence in the Church by pretending at odd moments that he is a monk at heart. But the monk, too, tends to realize that he is not an ethereal, unworldly being, nor yet a kind of glorified canon appointed to chant the office and teach school; that he too can discover the real meaning of his vocation by drawing closer to the simplicity and labor of the layman, which is his own traditional lot.

The Little Brothers of Jesus, founded by Charles de Foucauld, whose lives are much like those of the worker priests of the Mission de France, have in them definite elements of this "lay monasticism" in its good sense, and by their influence they are causing a rethinking of traditional monasticism in the ancient

Orders. In any case there is a renewed emphasis on the fact that ordinary life with its work, its insecurity and its inevitable sacrifices is for the Christian just as much part of the "sacred" realm as anything else, because, like everything else, it has been consecrated to God by the Incarnation, the Death and the Resurrection of Jesus Christ.

The real problem of a "clerical" Church is that it not only claims to mediate the light and holiness of God to the world, but it also implicitly sets itself squarely in between the Christian and the world, and we are seldom clear whether she is there as a defense, a barrier, or a mediator. In any case, the result is that the Christian is maintained, to some extent, in an attitude of passivity and tutelage. In order to "be a Christian" he has to let himself be protected against the world and kept "out of the world" by his Church. His daily plunges into the world are of course inevitable and they are tolerated, on condition that they are not what he "really means." What he "really means" is to save his soul by keeping himself, in his interior intention, aloof from the world in which, unfortunately, he has to give a great deal of time and attention to making a living.

This is a falsification and distortion of the true Gospel perspective about "the world," and it results in deplorable ambiguities. For one thing, this attitude ends by practically short-circuiting the real energy that the Christian (priest or layman) could conceivably put into his witness and his service in the world. The Christian, like Christ, is sent into the world to bear witness to the love of the Father for the world and for man, and to help man be redeemed by Christ. To say that man is redeemed "from the world" by Christ is to say that he is redeemed from the sinful use of created things and from the great complex of illusions and obsessions which organize human activity in the service of power, greed, lust, cruelty, hatred, egoism, and inhumanity. This is "the world" in the worst sense of the word (see I John 2:15). But to assume that all human and temporal existence, all work, all social life, all sexual and procreative love, all technology, all forms of human knowledge, recreation, art, and trade are by their very nature damnable and "worldly" is to remove them from the power and influence of Christ and His Church.

Marx was not far wrong when he diagnosed a certain decadent religiosity as a means of keeping man alienated from himself and from the world in which he lived and worked. Such alienation from reality was very effective in making man a serviceable instrument of others who used him for their own ends. And, we might add, these were strictly worldly ends. Hence to cut man off from the reality of his own life, his own work, and himself, by suggesting that these realities are all in some way vile is in fact not to redeem and rescue him but simply to enslave him more thoroughly to the forces that use his world, and him in it, for immoral and selfish ends. The most cogent argument against a spurious unworldliness is that it is in actual fact very effective in serving "the world" in the worst sense. The Christian who is unworldly only in this particular sense becomes an innocent cooperator in the work of degrading the world and submitting it still further to the forces of evil and of greed.

Worse than that, he may be in hypocritical connivance with "worldliness" in its most deplorable sense. History shows plenty of examples of Christians who have, with the "right intention," wrought great wrong, and experience shows that once one has theoretically admitted the primacy of the spiritual over the "worldly" and tacitly added the admission that one is not yet capable of the spiritual so he might as well make the best of the worldly, the result has been a much more radical and godless secularization of the secular. Those today who call for the recognition of the "sacred" possibilities within the "secular" realm itself are in fact summoning the Christian layman to a much more heroic and radical commitment than would be demanded of him by a life of unprincipled "secularity" during the week redeemed by a half hour of distracted sacredness on Sunday, tinged with regret that one was not cut out to be a Carmelite or a Trappist.

Another and more cogent example of the effects of a spirituality that divorces the "spiritual life" from everyday social reality: Father Berrigan remembers occasions when racial justice was preached to Southern congregations, including the instance when part of the congregation got up and walked out, not without insults (one devout soul left with the shout: "If I miss Mass this Sunday, it is *your fault*"). There seems to be a rather general belief in the South that the whole race question has nothing whatever to do with religion or with Christianity. The business of the pastor or of the preacher is to talk about Jesus, "so why are they shouting about civil rights and getting everybody upset?" There is sincere indignation about this irruption of base and world distractions into the tranquillity of the sacred—a tranquillity guaranteed by the fact that in the sacred realm of interiority things are more what you like them to be, whereas in the world of brutal and secular fact they have a tendency to resist manipulation and to require more distracting forms of attention.

There is a "fruitful ambiguity" in the book's title, *No More Strangers*. The reader will recall the Pauline context. It comes in the liturgy for the Feasts of the Apostles. "You are no more strangers and sojourners but fellow citizens with the saints and members of the household of God" (Ephesians 2:19). In the Pauline text the "stranger" is he who is estranged from Christ and from the people of God. But in this book there are also allusions to the problem that the Christian has become alienated and estranged from the contemporary world. This alienation, this estrangement are due, we have seen, precisely to a superficial and distorted understanding of the "unworldliness" to which we are summoned by the Gospel. The New Testament certainly demands that the Christian be converted from "the world" to "Christ and His Church," since his vocation is to follow Christ "out of this world to the Father," together with the new Israel, the Chosen People. But "the world" in this context means the whole realm of greed, power, lust, selfishness, hatred, and inhumanity. It certainly does not mean the world of everyday reality, of common duty, of work, of play, of sorrow and joy, the world in which man is called to work out his destiny as a son of God.

Hence it is important to spell out the contradiction that is implied in a false spirituality which, in making a man a stranger to the everyday realities of life willed for mankind by God, actually estranges him from Christ. That is why modern apostles insist on the need for Christians to love the world. Love for the world in this sense does not mean love for power, for selfish greed and lust, but love for the common lot and task of man. Indeed it means above all love for man himself, and thereby love for Christ. Today we can see the urgency of restoring this true perspective, of casting aside the outworn formulas of a false unworldliness that has no other result than to divide man within himself and deliver him over all the more completely to the greeds and hatred of "the world." True Christian unworldliness is not a rejection of man or of God's creation; it is a firm and ardent faith which is strong enough to find Christ in man and in man's world. It can see a sacred meaning and a divine message in the secular needs and struggles of twentieth-century man. It can see Christ suffering in the peoples who starve, who seek their just rights, their freedom, their chance to develop and build themselves a new civilization. *This awareness of Christ in the world today is the basic intuition upon which the work of renewal and* aggiornamento *must be built.* To be a stranger to the needs of our fellow man and to the hopes and perils of this moment of history is to be a stranger to Christ Himself, and no amount of interiority can supply for this lack of Christian insight.

Such is the message which this book utters with impassioned conviction. It will teach us that our mission as Catholics in the world today is not a mission merely to consolidate our own position and establish our own prestige, to protect our institutions amid the insecurities of a world in full revolution. It is a mission to witness to Christ in this changing world, to see Him in modern man, so that we recognize that our duty is more to our fellow man, whether he be a Christian or not, than to our own advantage and prestige. We do not know what the future may bring, but we know that our job is to face it with courage and hope and share our hope with our fellow man. We have more to do than sing hymns while the ship goes down.

January 1965   THOMAS MERTON

NO MORE STRANGERS

1. The Nature of Christian Witness

What is the pertinence of Christian witness to men today? Within the scheme of Redemption, is it fully as important to give Christian witness as to receive it? Can the witness of the Christian, properly conceived and executed, make a difference in some of the more critical areas of current human relationships? In an attempt to analyze the relevance of Christianity to the world situation, questions like these arise as a radical point of departure. It would seem that the answers would constitute a very large share of what the Church must say to modern man.

The presence of Christ in His Redemption argues to humanity's need for Our Lord's witness about Himself, and argues further to a voluntary acceptance of that witness as a condition for partnership in Him. It is revealing to notice that John, the Saviour's herald, "came as a witness, to bear witness concerning the light, that all men might believe through him" (John 1:7). For "John bore witness concerning him, and cried, 'This was he of whom I said . . .'" (John 1:15). Later, Christ perfected the declaration of John by applying it to Himself. "And the Father himself, who has sent me, has borne witness to me . . . I have come in the name of my Father, and you do not receive me . . ." (John 5: 37,43). At this point, John's witness is accomplished, the Father approves the words and works of His Son. Our Lord affirmed this as He healed the cripple at the Probatic Pool, ". . . the Son can do nothing of himself, but only what he sees the Father doing. For whatever he does, this the Son also does in like manner" (John

5:19). The unity of nature shared by Christ and His Father is the single source of the unity of truth and effort in the Sacred Humanity. Christ proved His mission by witnessing to the truth of the Father in Himself.

Subsequently, Christians receive from Christ and His Church the essential role of witness. Following the Resurrection, the mandate Christ gave to the Twelve was that of witness. ". . . you shall be witnesses for me in Jerusalem, and in all Judea and Samaria and even to the very ends of the earth" (Acts 1:8). That they understood Him very well is proved by the repeated use that John and Paul made of the same expression of "witness" in their writings as evidence that they looked upon the role of witness as standing at the heart of Christian existence. Finally, the Apostles drew attention to Jesus by the testimony of their blood, for they regarded martyrdom to be the supreme evidence of their Lord, the first martyr.

The theological roots of "witness" go deep into the Trinitarian Life, and to the very existence of God. In creation, God bore witness to Himself, to His Thought and to His Love, because of His desire to communicate the limitless goodness that is Himself. The reality of man is a witness to His maker, insofar as human nature is a created expression of the Divine Nature, and of the Three Persons in man's power of thought and word and love. Again, the Redemption is a witness to God, showing once more the paramount concern of the Divine for the human; showing that God did not shrink from embracing the human condition to prove this concern; showing finally, that God would even die to testify that His own death to sin would break the power of death if man would recognize Him as the Life.

The Church bears witness to God in that she is the prolongation of Christ; more than this, the Church is the witness of God, because she is Christ in His members. Lastly, the

Eucharist bears witness to all of the above, since it creates anew, announces the Redemption, gives life to the Church, and feeds the Christian; all for one purpose, to witness to the Death and Resurrection of Christ as salvation and everlasting life.

With regard to the meaning of Christian witness, it is not difficult to predicate several startling parallels between the contemporary Church and the Church of the early Christian era. Then, as now, the problem was largely one of exclusiveness. Early Christian thought centered about Jewish tradition, and Jewish theology practically controlled it. Despite the admonitions of Christ that the whole world must be engaged, despite the opposition of Paul, there was a bogging down into the old order, and a view of mission that had little to do with universalism. Was not Christ Himself a Jew, and did He not say that He had come for "the lost sheep of the house of Israel" (St. Matthew 15:24)? We have here a Christianity still wrestling with the pangs of birth, devoted to the temple, obeying the Mosaic Law and offering sacrifices in Jerusalem. It was only the power of the Spirit and the instrumentality of Paul that was to break this stalemate, that was to impel the first Christians toward a universal witness and a Church that was truly Catholic.

In considerable measure, we have strong similarities to this outlook alive in the Church today. The word "Catholic" has been understood for a long time in a dangerously ambiguous sense as primarily denoting a member of a religious society, whose expression has assumed worldwide dimensions. In this context, the Catholic is one who participates in a wide-flung institution, which radiates from the administrative and authoritative core of Rome, which waits upon an authority for its initiative and mandate. With most Christians, consciousness of "being" the Church is either never acquired or is tenuously held in the dim recollection of a rare and unusual sermon or is lost in the entanglements of a tense and complex life. In this situation, if anything further were needed to relieve the conscience and to discharge one from his responsibility, there is the evidence of Church institutional life everywhere, those secure and impressive pockets of Christian vitality where Church professionals do her work of education and service, where religion has built up the Kingdom of God, stable and high, within the walls. Exclusiveness in such circumstances is the normal temptation and tendency. From a theology of the synagogue and the Law, we have evolved a theology of the institution and its law. Christian witness, its direction and provision, lies somewhere beyond the pale, where it may be tolerated but is seldom received and welcomed.

Some breakthrough is being achieved against the old pattern of things. The world is impinging on the ecclesiastical institution far too powerfully and variously to be ignored and put off. Moreover, the layman is aware of the dichotomy between his religious and his secular experience and it leads him to question institutional validity. Finally, a tremendous impulse of renewal has been engendered by the Vatican Council, through which the Spirit is reforming the Church according to the Christian ideal and according to human need. Yet, despite such hopes, one must still think in terms of the threefold revolution in population, technology, and human rights, in terms of the cold war, poverty, and Christian division, in terms of an upheaval of values and a burgeoning of anticipation whose momentous speed is striking a response from every human chord and condition. Confronted with such explosive world changes, the quest for the radical Christian position daily becomes more urgent. Modern man refuses to restrict the pace of his expectations to the progress of religious reform. In some cases, man will refuse to anticipate the Church's blessing upon his life and hopes; in others, he will decide that the Church's sanction would make no difference even if it came; in others, he will simply find it impossible to wait. Immediacy is the rallying cry, and many have decided that technology, politics, and sociology are the panaceas.

II

What is the quality of Christian witness today, and what forms best characterize it? As might be expected, it has taken a wide variety of expression, ranging from the heroic to the safe. In lay circles (it is with the layman that we are most concerned) the reality of life commitment grows, both at home and abroad. There are those who have pledged themselves to the interests of the Church in action outside of the Church structure. There are men and women who are helping to revitalize the extra-parochial and parish apostolates. There are in average parishes the Catholic masses who, in matters of a positive Christian witness, have yet to be heard from. Finally, there are those who are on the move in different stages of decision and development. And though the Christian apostolate is as diversified and complex as life itself, it is no less true that those who are lapsed and uncommitted often present the greatest challenge to the reality of Christian witness. Among these can be found not only the poor and the racially ostracized, but victims of all kinds, whose shackles may include wealth, psuedo-intellectualism, status-seeking, and neuroticism. It is simply not possible to reach these people in depth with the saving message of the Gospel unless a far broader apostolic base is established, unless the layman is given his work and the freedom and training necessary to pursue it.

Judging from the sobering absence of significant numbers of lay apostles in the Church, there is also a decided confusion as to how Christian witnesses are to be formed. This confusion is marked and widespread, plainly visible on all levels of Church education—in the caliber of liturgical participation and preaching, in the choice and number of parish lay organizations, and in the quality of apostolic training. It is possible that general embarrassment would follow any inquiry on the parish level as to what is being done to produce the authentic layman. The history of most American parishes speaks of many things, but particularly of a fearful dearth of motivation, awareness, and sophistication in the kind of social experience that will move the lay Christian from apathy to interest, from inactivity to initiative. Without being aware of it, our parishes have very often supported an apostolate that is no apostolate at all, because it possesses so little of the essential quality of evangelism. Without being aware of it, we have been supporting one of the most powerful forms of social control, simply because our conception of religion has caused a neutrality of conformism. And we have never gauged what this might mean to our neighbor, or to one larger community.

What must be done, therefore, to realize the aim of Christian formation, which is, as Yves de Montcheuil calls it, the "obtaining of free acts from men"? What is needed to convince the lay Christian, of whatever age or condition, that he stands between God and the world as Christ's ambassador, that his mind and heart and hands are Christ's, and that his essential gift is himself as a force of peace and reconciliation? What is needed to discipline the Christian mind and heart that service of neighbor becomes a *sine qua non* of life, a central and integrating principle? What is needed to instill in the Christian that rare type of intelligence and love which consistently attacks personal egoism, thereby making charity a form of consciousness? To a dangerous degree, our parishes are incapable of answering these questions, either academically or structurally. In fact, they are often not able to diagnose why they are not centers of formation for a witness of this kind.

It is not our purpose here to offer a comprehensive analysis of the training given to priests and religious, a training which, in fact, often inhibits the competence of priests to empathize with the lay world. At this point, one could usefully suggest that the formal training given to priests, sisters, and brothers is decidedly monastic in nature. It prepares them for the relative isolation of institutional life and gives them certain skills toward making the institution "work." The spirituality taught in his context is personal rather than social; the introduction to life experience negligible or, at best, of a speculative rather than practical nature. The imagination is given little opportunity for expansion, being bounded by preparation for the limited realities of one's future work. Pragmatic attitudes in this atmosphere become deeply rooted, for they are the logical corollary of a conviction that the Church faces God as a hierarchical-sacramental system, whose institutional aspects are very nearly everything. Though it is not stated quite so bluntly, the formative ethos is this: The Church mission is the Church institution. Such an introduction to their witness can hardly educate the priest and, even less, the sister or brother for a penetration of lay life, for provisions of understanding it as it is, of explaining it to one's self, or of offering to it the best directives for its own fulfillment. Not knowing the world as it is and, in the ordinary scheme of things, being inhibited from learning enough of life, the priest or religious could hardly be thought capable of presenting the full meaning of the world to the layman.

III

The question of Christian witness is, largely speaking, a question of man's growth in Christ. This crucial matter has often been neglected, or if it is dealt with at all, it is treated in an unrealistic and impractical manner. There is no point in glossing over the difficulty here. Human growth, even in the best of situations, is a painful business, and great care must be taken that the person is not overwhelmed by prospects that seem unmanageable or impossible. Growth in Christ must therefore be presented as a normal condition of life, one analogous to physical maturation. Moreover, it should be spoken of as the essential way toward a fully human life, as the necessary qualification for personal mastery, and above all, as a true sign of adulthood in Christ's Kingdom. Conversely, moral stagnation, or any sort of leveling off in one's relationship with God, should be exposed as a source of fallacy and illusion, including a crystallized ego, emotional immaturity, vulnerability to error and myth, impotence of will, social myopia, superficiality of friendship, and escapism. It is the experience of priests who are profoundly engaged with laymen that any appeal to legitimate self-interest, any presentation of the way toward true freedom, engages the lay imagination, enkindles hope of betterment, and creates an interior expansion favorable to the action of the Holy Spirit.

Perhaps two things are accomplished by this initial discussion of human consciousness as a seedbed of growth: the person gets both a taste of what he is, and a promise of what he can be. By it, the distinction between self and egoism is clarified, and soil has been prepared for an enlightened and beneficial choice.

It is quite impossible to expect the growth of man to truly human stature without reference to Our Lord. For the Christian, humanity must mean Christ, both in growth and in the realization of adulthood. In the Redemption, Christ took our life to Himself, and the single task of life is responsive and loving reaction to that act, man must now put on Christ. In this view Our Lord becomes the first and final definition of the human, the Holy One Who creates, saves and awaits us, Who would, in the process, give us new life and liberty. We must all reach out toward Him through faith and love, recognize and serve Him in the lives of His brothers, pass through Him in death. There is no other way to the Father. His Humanity, perfect and unstained, through which the Word of God has entered history and sworn Himself to the human lot, would be the unifying energy in man's nature, once divided within itself, the victim of its own violent fears and divisions. As St. Augustine wrote: "We who were sundered and at enmity, by reason of our sensuality and the diverse desires and uncleanness of our sins, being cleansed by the Mediator, should set out together (with Him) toward that same blessedness, and being forged together into one mind by the fire of love, are united, not in our common nature alone, but by the bond of a common love."

In His human life He took us up, the burden of His loving kindness; He lived the common life of man, at the same time transcending our life by way of the promise of immortality, the sign of what He could make of us. He was "made like unto men . . . appearing in the form of man" (Philippians 2:7) yet no man ever spoke as this Man, no man served as Him, no man died as He died. Blaise Pascal wrote of Christ: "Without possessions and having produced nothing which could be called science, He is of the order of saintliness. He made no invention; He did not reign; but He was humble, patient, saintly—saintly before God, terrible in the eyes of demons, sinless." He Who was God became man; every word or act of His life spoke of His love for us. Finally, whatever else could be said of His Passion and Death, it came upon Him because He was willing to pay the price of heroic love, willing to embrace us as we were, willing to expose Himself to the attacks of a nature so at variance with itself that it had become a force of destruction, both of itself and of any man who would unmask its futility and waste.

Gethsemane was Christ's first experience in a total identification with the rebellious humanity of every age, and the confrontation would so unnerve Him that He would plead for release. From it, Calvary was the summit of His self-denial, the last and most excellent example of a love that would prove His undoing by impelling Him to death, the woeful and glorious moment of His final union with sinful man, who would kill Him, and in turn, die to sin through the Saviour's blood. The men who caused His death, then, were those He took to death with Him, and they became those who rose with Him. From that point on, everything in human life, whether in time or in eternity, would rest upon the reply to that question of His: "What think you of the Christ?" Perhaps the tragedy of today is not precisely that men answer wrongly to this question. It is rather that they do not know how to answer, or that they are so seldom asked.

Christ, then, was witness to God, but He was also witness to man. To emphasize a series of truisms (neglected because they are so true): He became man and universal man, because in the economy of Redemption, *He was now Man.* He stood for absolute fidelity to the contract made with Man, that is, with Himself. For it was the hope of Christ, a hope that in His Resurrection became a reality, that when God had proved His fidelity to man, then man would see the possibility of fidelity to God. The implications for ourselves are clear. It is that Christian witness incarnates and projects the meidatorship of Christ, His obedience to His Father, and His commitment to man. Our witness must introduce into the human order the truth of Christ's present existence, His present Law, and His present Redemption in such a way that no man need feel alone, without guidance or hope. Witness means standing for Christ in the midst of human pain, perplexity, and inertia in such a way that alleviation becomes real, understanding is relished, and spiritual growth becomes imperative. The Christian witness, if he knows what he is about, is one who can preserve a healthy tension between the stature of his own person and the hesitant gropings of another, even while preserving in the other the necessary ingredient of hope. So it is that he can extend compassion without paternalism, and service without self-righteousness or didacticism.

It would seem that honesty requires one to underscore (at the risk of protesting the obvious) that the object of witness is man. Without man and his fallen state, there would be no reason for God's present order of things, for the Incarnation, or for Christ's redemptive plan. In spite of our theoretical acceptance of this truth, we often subscribe to a persistent and paradoxical Christian heresy which takes as the point of departure a witness to God without witness to man, which attempts to live Christian truth without communicating it, which claims love of God, but fears love of man. It is a heresy which has long cloaked itself as a religious and moral system, but which is, in reality, a selfish and pragmatic ethic. Its emphasis upon worship at the expense of the works of mercy (Emmanuel Cardinal Suhard observes that this is a criterion of religious decline) is evidence that we unconsciously seek in religion a divine sanction for personal pride, a climate suitable for sentiment, a philosophy that will pad and cushion one from the demands of life, or allow us to deal with only its more palatable forms, justifying a contact with life that is peculiarly detached and contemptuous.

Such an outlook has bred a system in which the following facts stand out. The institution supersedes the person, because it offers tools for ready communication with God, while proposing at the same time a simple, undemanding code to cover association with men. Principles assume a convenient vagueness and can be promptly denied or adroitly rationalized when they do not fit personal desires. Subjectivism is regarded as invulnerable to proof or experience, ready to be projected into the community under the force of precept, or even counsel. Rules are central, but such a mentality will ignore their underlying spirit, for to such an outlook, issues must be kept

black or white—the browns and grays are dimissed as nonexistent, or as conspiracies of the far left. Change is received
with apprehension and suspicion, for there is an assumption
operating that the personal world is the best possible world—
one to be kept as immovable as the personal pattern of life.
One's approach to the human community will be unilateral to
the degree that judgment as to its course and aspirations becomes very nearly obsessive, as the groping attempts of others
to accept and improve life are met with fear and castigation.
God and other men are pressed into service of the self; and
life becomes a recital of proving to others how unenlightened
they are. Finally, men committed to such a system often
espouse a religiously and politically right position which tends
to contradict the hopes of man, his human rights, human
liberty, human needs, and even on occasion, the magisterium
of the Church, the Gospels themselves. For one's self and
one's possessions must be protected at all costs, or the agencies
which protect one's self and one's possessions must be preserved.

By way of contrast, the Christian witness will not seek for
himself the dangerous luxury of any appraisal of Christ that
Christ Himself has not taught. The Gospels and the Church
speak too strongly to him for that. Nor should his worship
detract from service of neighbor—it rather prepares him for
such service. He sees Christian institutions as helpful and
effective as long as they are well used; but he is not wedded to
them as absolutes which are above evaluation and, in some
cases, above replacement. The Law he views as a thing of
mighty importance, as indeed Christ viewed it; yet the Christian knows that unless legality has a base in love and is interpreted by love it can become a weapon to club and cripple
people, instead of encouraging them and supplying guidelines
for conscience. The world may challenge his values, indict his
life, cause him suffering, demand from him unceasingly his

time, effort, and money, but he still loves it as the matrix of his humanity, the preserve of his Church, the home where he is born into life and into God. So he will take from the world with gratitude and give to it with largess of spirit, knowing that even as he nourishes his being on its elements, he must renew it by the gift of his spirit.

Again, the labels of right or center or left will acquire meaning and command the adherence of Christians only as they meet the test of the Gospels, the mind of the Church, and the requirements of mankind. God is his Father whom he serves in other sons; history is a charge and stewardship which must be administered through dependence upon his Father and through faithful bonds with other men. The Christian witness is the man, finally, who sees his life as a redemptive fact, as a definition which God Himself has made:

> That man is a Catholic (Christian), who opens himself to all and allows the universal love of the Lord to resound in his heart. He is a Catholic who, when he remembers the mercy of Christ toward him, becomes merciful, that is to say, overwhelmed with distress, whatever form that distress may take. He is a Catholic who instinctively rejects everything that is a source of division, who cannot meet anyone without tirelessly seeking out an area of agreement. He is a Catholic who sees in each man not the social category to which he belongs, not the label which is applied to him, of unbeliever or Protestant or Jew or Communist, but the brother for whom Christ died and who has been placed in his path in order to receive his love. He is a Catholic who, through humility, has made himself poor in spirit and is always ready to welcome those who are deprived, whether it be of material goods or the light of faith.*

* Bishop Gérard Huyghe, Bishop of Arras, Pastoral Letter, May 14, 1962.

IV

The formation of Christian witness is a task as long as life itself, a task which implies many avenues of initiative and influence. But generally, its aim is a developed view of the historical Christ, of His unbreakable link with contemporary man as he builds up Christ's Body. The formation must begin with the awareness that within time, Our Lord achieved an effect which surpasses time. Through the Church, Christ's Death, Resurrection, and Ascension are the *fact* of every age, injected into history through Word, sacrament, and man. There are presently among us diverse epiphanies of Christ: the Word of Truth that teaches us within the Church; the birth, nourishment, and healing that He accomplishes through the sacraments; the degree of fullness or deprivation of Himself that He shows us in the face of our neighbor. The first virtue must necessarily be one of faith; it must be the hard and ennobling struggle to look upon the world of Church and man as God sees it—in the all-encompassing glance which accepts the realities of human nobility and degradation, contrast and paradox. ". . . We suffer tribulation, but we are not distressed; we are sore pressed, but we are not destitute; we endure persecution, but we are not forsaken; we are cast down, but we do not perish; always bearing about in our body the dying Jesus, so that the life also of Jesus may be made manifest in our bodily frame" (II Corinthians 4:8-10).

This faculty of active faith makes the Christian witness the indispensable leaven and benign catalyst in society. In the divine plan, it is both his role and capability to direct the hopes of mankind, mature its adolescence, and temper its violence. Therefore, both his intellectual and instinctual resources will help him to perceive issues which thinking men everywhere are perceiving: the classical alternatives to the Bomb, the therapeutic and providential struggle of the Negro, the challenging and reproachful presence of the Marxist, the reforming contributions of Protestants and Orthodox. He will support, with rationality and articulate explanation, the need for international and world government; and he will be impressed with the damaging irrelevancy of nationalism. He will be pained by the inequities of wealth and poverty; he will work for a political and economic system which will place limits on the greed of the rich while eliminating the distress of the poor. He will regard responsibility of leadership as the greatest need of his community, and will toil tirelessly in the molding of others of like conviction. He will be a good citizen, but his primary allegiance will be to God and world; and when he reflects upon patriotism, it will be in these terms. Apostolate, movement, neighborhood, and job: these are the areas where he meets the world, while his prayer, effort, and suffering invigorate all men, circling the globe and penetrating every life within it.

Generally, it can be said that the difference between the ordinary Christian and the Christian witness is a different relationship to reality and a different capability of grasping it. For the first, the objective world is more or less seen in a glass darkly—moral insight is rare, egoism is impulsive, effort is disliked, suffering is feared. On the other hand, the witness begins by assenting to reality and he has a wholesome uneasiness over the insufficiency of his grasp of it. But he affirms its presence and accepts his responsibility of seeing it more clearly, knowing that public change will depend largely on what he is and becomes.

Any education toward Christian witness then, must give primary attention to the fact that what one sees is often not the reality of things at all; that one's view of life has been engendered by a misreading of personal and fundamental needs. Thus affective life may be undisciplined and grasping; mental activity and will power may be weakened by emotionalism. It is precisely at the point of self-apprehension that the ruinous cycle must be broken—by whatever means possible the person must be confronted with reality. The shock of such an encounter can be made bearable by the reality of Christ, Whose perfection we are commanded to incorporate through the mission of the Church to mankind, which is ours as well; through the corporate agony of the Body of Christ, for which we bear responsibility; through the brother, whose destiny is intermingled with our own. The object of this stage of formation will be to implant an enlightened understanding, which will prompt a profound dissatisfaction with one's human state in the encounter with the powerful realities of the spiritual order.

This initial period of understanding and honesty is a very crucial one. Within the scope of the spiritual life and the apostolic witness it is comparable to the plaintive and shrinking helplessness of childhood. New vistas of truth and self-realization are very attractive, but paying the price exacted for them is feared. Both present and future have lost their apparent security. The situation is often reducible to the question of leaving the known for the unknown. Though fragmented and rather pointless, one's present life is known, and, to a degree, is looked upon as secure and predictable. On the contrary, the unknown involvement with Christ means a change—not only acceptance of new values but such a mastery of these values that one can implant them in other lives. As a further complication, immediate relationships are under strain—wife, family, and friends are drawn into the abruptness of personal change. There is, therefore, the complexity, confusion, and pain of the personal phase, plus the insecurity of new association with others. The emotions are bound to protest against such as assault, their dominance being threatened perhaps for the first time in a serious way.

This is an exacting and significant period therefore, about

evenly divided between peaks of enthusiasm and harassments of depression. An intoxicating freedom of spirit may be felt; new horizons of influence have suddenly appeared; human relationships become provocative and enriching; energy appears to be boundless. On the other hand, misunderstanding will be common; people will prove obtuse and recalcitrant; personal perplexities will be compounded by public confusion and pain. It is common that during this time one grows deeply anxious in the thought that he is the victim of inexorable pressures from within and from without. His aspirations are caught between personal impotence and the hostile, static attitude of the world. It would be an error in method to meet the impasse with banter or harshness. An error, because no one in such a plight is in a position to appreciate wit or judgment—his situation is simply too painful. What he needs is the help of others, in the form of receptivity, patience, and an empathy which arises from deep Christian compassion. It is often the mistake of directors in such a situation to neglect to listen, and, instead, to indulge in a monologue of personal experience and direct advice. But it is not the director's experience that is the point here, nor is even good advice always helpful. Rather, the experience actually being undergone must be clarified, slowly and step by step, with the help of the silent understanding of a man of experience, who knows that his primary role is helping the layman to understand himself.

Inevitably, it becomes necessary to reflect upon the structures that mature the layman. Such organizations are of critical need today (as Pope John so often remarked)—they are the most striking evidence of a true lay community within the Church; they are also dependable centers for Christian formation. It is true that there are growing numbers of Christian witnesses today who insist on a rather evident separation from present lay structures, preferring rather to serve the world with others who share their humanitarian convictions. But even in their case it goes without saying that they must draw both discernment and strength from the larger community of the Church; their sponsorship still comes from the mind of the Church and it is still supported by the sacraments. But nonetheless, apart from this type of witness, the lay structure is of prime importance—both for reasons of the community that it offers to its members and for the service that it can extend to the larger society.

One rather subtle danger that comes immediately to the fore in the beginnings of lay organizational life is the question of mystique. Why is the organization being started and what will be its relationship to society? These concerns are of profound importance. There are lay groups which have unwittingly succumbed to a mollified institutionalism. Some will offer an interminable moral training, as though engagement with the problems of people had no contribution to make in spiritual formation. Others will concentrate on the fringe activities of the social apostolate—retreats, study clubs, the liturgical movement—in an intelligent confusion of ends and means. One sees operating here a kind of lay monasticism, another design of the pious elite—esoteric, academic, introverted, and sometimes more apt to direct vital energies away from witness than toward it. One criterion to test the validity of a lay group is its apostolic objectives; they alone indicate caliber of membership, pertinence of training, quality of leadership, and social consciousness. An apostolate which is immature and radically removed from the main currents of human movement and aspiration invariably suggests that its members have been "bought off" by the institution and anesthetized in their role by clerical condescension.

In any program of formation, there is also the clerical view of the layman to be considered. Clerics who are convinced that lay leadership is the Church's greatest need (there are not many of these) are, notwithstanding, usually rather ill-prepared to put their convictions to work. Being the product of a seminary which, if it is typical, did not study the layman either theoretically or practically, the cleric comes to the ministry with good will but without requisite knowledge or experience. It is common that they know few laymen engaged in domestic or foreign service; they have little acquaintance with lay groups and apostolic techniques; they have not yet begun to formulate and communicate a lay theology; they have been taught little or nothing of counseling or spiritual direction; their ignorance of lay solutions to social issues is quite complete; they know neither the layman nor what he is meant to do nor his potential for doing it. In addition (as if these debilities were not crippling enough), there is the common encounter with misunderstanding and opposition from pastors and superiors, who in their turn, have come from a training even more deprived in relation to the layman. In this context it is the rare priest who has the spiritual and mental fiber to grapple with such difficulties, to weather them and to test them, while learning a mode of operation which is faithful to the layman, even as it preserves a firm sense of obedience.

Supposing, however, a measure of freedom in work with the layman (this is more possible than is commonly believed), the first step is now possible. The priest must now undertake his own education, which may mean the abandonment of many stereotyped ways of thought that have crept into consciousness during the years of training. Some of these might be expressed in these propositions: theology can be taught to laymen by the Seminary method; laymen, by nature and role, are priest's helpers; social witness can be effective only after protracted spiritual training; the lay apostolate is necessarily a parish apostolate; decisions about the training of laymen and, even more, their work is primarily a clerical matter. Upon reflection, it must be admitted that a seminary education directed solely or even primarily to the sacraments and catechetics can hardly avoid a deep-seated conditioning of a cleri-cal view of lay life. This clerical view often takes the form of regarding the layman as sort of an uncassocked and informal reproduction of the priest, with a primary responsibility to the institution of the Church rather than to society. Such a fixation would make of the layman a clerical arm, whose mis-sion would wholly depend on a clerical mandate.

All this is, of course, very far from the truth of things, which include the layman's right to society as the field of action, as the area of his true competency. And when we speak of the layman's relationship to the ordained priesthood, it is not exaggeration to say that the priest needs the apostolic layman fully as much as the layman needs him, though in a different way. In the nature of things then, the priest's rela-tionship with the laity must never be patronizing, never less than adult, never lacking in gratitude and respect. If anything, the priest must interpret his relationship to the layman in terms of what the layman needs from him to fulfill himself within the Church. This relationship is quite identical with the nature of the lay role, considering it in a real and apostolic sense.

Next, there are Church institutions to consider. The way that we regard them and the stability and permanence that we seek for them show that we generally consider them not only impervious to change but, somehow, an argument against change. These attitudes have their own consequences. One of them is an image of the Church which generally seeks to affect the contemporary world only through the Church institution. In turn, the institution seeks, not the transforma-tion of the human community, but a kind of Catholic precinct in society, which operates there under a covenant of "live and let live" with the community that tolerates it. Such objectives might have been defensible in the immigrant Church, where the rights of existence and acceptance were vitally necessary concerns. They are far less defensible now. There is some truth indeed in the statement that the mission of the American Church has been more of an exchange between clergymen and Church institutions than a dialogue between Church and society.

It is most difficult to expect from our layman the type of witness that society so grievously needs as long as his action is restricted within institutional limits. This is at least part of the frustration which laymen feel today. As a rule the religious establishment currently sees itself as mediator between men of the Church and men of society, as something of a substitute priest, which if it does not control the thought and actions of Christians, it at least very heavily influences them. Because of the institution, therefore, the prophetic voice of the Church is frequently stifled before it can find expression, or it is muffled within walls or controlled by institutional ethos. It is for these reasons that the laity is expected to promote the institutional good of the Church, instead of being in direct touch with modern life in all its forms. Ideally and reasonably, we should look upon our structures as tools which assist both service and evangelism. This is hardly the case however. Instead, present structures tend to dictate to us the terms of local witness, and even the manner in which it is to be carried out.

The result of this can hardly be other than inadequate and even disastrous, since the institution tends to absorb more and more attention and energy to itself. Controlling men and resources as it does, it is often insensitive, irrational, and immobile, both as an abstraction and a reality. It is little wonder, therefore, that we find it so difficult to adapt our parishes to the needs of social worship, or our schools to education for the community and its needs. It is little wonder, in consequence, that priests are not generally on open terms with an open laity; or that the full potential of our sisters is seldom realized, bound as they are to convent, school, and hospital, where both rule and institution contrive to hem them in, and to demand all their energy; or that even the best of our laity, people of superb artistic and professional potential, are offered a choice which is unrealistic and self-defeating—service within the structure or no service at all.

Institutional realities exercise, by and large, a strong dominion over Catholics, both religious and lay. They also keep at a distance the object of mediation, the world, and they react too slowly to demands and needs. Thus, in many places, our institutions operate in near proximity to poverty and human wreckage, while they numbly continue to cater to a privileged class. They often turn away from a changing parochial situation with disgust and suspicion, as though minority groups were invaders or trespassers on sacred ground. On a large and significant scale, they assimilate our best religious—into a life of patterned and undiscerning hard work, so that they become silent drudges in the system. On many occasions, moreover, our institutions are expensive, and materially burdensome to the Christian people, because of ill design, because of inefficiency, or because their raison d'etre is obsolescent or superficial. Bishop John King Mussio has written accurately of the general inadequacy of the American parish structure and the unwholesome focus upon the parish school. One is not far wrong in stating that many American parishes seem to exist only to serve a parish school, which in numerous cases controls the priests, sisters, and laity, holding them to an uncompromising and unquestioning relationship. Sometimes, indeed, it will take the moral and material resources of several thousand Catholics, several priests, and many sisters to keep in operation a tiny institution of 400 children, where the predictable, unexamined work goes forward, turning out young Catholics who are youthful replicas of their parents, faithful to the sacraments, but apostolically ignorant and unambitious.

In reference to these realities, it would be quite extravagant to look for an automatic renewal of Church institutions in terms of more intelligent and open use of them as missionary instruments. In fact, renewal will only come about after a major reform of seminaries, in addition to a general agreement on in-service training for present Church professionals. It seems reasonable to suppose that if there arises a more intensive overhaul of the Church institution (this seems not only necessary, but inevitable), the valid lay organization can hasten the process, since laymen can speak to the institution forcefully and truly whenever it fails to evaluate or to extrude and deploy its forces, or to learn its work from the ever-shifting human scene. Such a witness, it would seem, must be an essential contribution to the dialectic between Church and society—the layman is the reciprocal link between Christ and men. So he must speak to mankind of the Church, returning to speak to the Church of mankind.

V

The liturgy is Christ's own gift to the Church, it is fashioned to inject spiritual vitality into the Christian life, so that men may gain the necessary courage and strength for Christ's redemptive task. Yet the Mass and the Sacraments, if their effects are to be fully present in men, also depend on a sense of the sacred that partakes of the sacred with awareness and love. In such a way one comes to see himself in the full implications of redemptive responsibility. The Scriptures say: "without the shedding of blood there is no forgiveness" (Hebrews 9:22). We can apply the text to suggest that the Blood which is poured out upon our altars is offered so that men may undertake the hard and noble business of witness, with all its nuances of study and observation, of nonconformity and questioning, of compassion and hard work. From the liturgy, the Christian must absorb the testimony and dyna-

mism of Christ—he must accept His commission, and embark
with Christ on a work of healing and reclamation. The Mass
is destined, therefore, to usher the Christian into a life of
enlightenment and oblation, into sacrifice and self-consumma-
tion, into nourishment and determined, confident action. The
Sacrament of Penance is meant to reinstate us in integrity of
life by forgiving our past sins, and by guaranteeing our solidarity with the lives of all those who form the community of
Christ's hope. Undergirding all, and constantly active in the
work of reconciliation, baptism continues to fashion the new
man in the new creation of Christ. The growth of Christians
depends, in fact, on our realization that the Liturgy of Word
and Sacrament prolongs the experience of death and victory
into Christ's people—to be accepted and lived as a privilege
and as a ministry.

Prayer must also be developed as a support of sacramental
action, and as an integral aspect of the Christian mission. The
Lessons for the Feast of St. Mark offer us something explicit
about the nature of prayer: "Pray for one another, that you
may be saved. For the unceasing prayer of a just man is of
great avail" (James 5: 16). Our Lord in turn tells us: "But if
one of you asks his father for a loaf, will he hand him a stone?
or for a fish, will he for a fish hand him a serpent? or if he asks
for an egg, will he hand him a scorpion? Therefore, if you,
evil as you are, know how to give good gifts to your children,
how much more will your heavenly Father give the Good
Spirit to those who ask him!" (St. Luke 11:11-13). Many
things are clear from such advice—certainly the power of
confident faith and magnanimity in prayer, but also this fact:
If it is by ministry of the Spirit that awareness and social
reconciliation are possible in human life, is it not consistent
that the Spirit be implored to stand more powerfully at our
side? Does it not seem to follow that if one be struggling for
peace, for interracial justice, for Christian unity, he should

also appeal to the Spirit—that He reduce the causes of war, that He lead men to brotherhood, that He strengthen Christian leaders everywhere. In such a way, the prayer of Christ for human unity and peace is specified strenuously, perseveringly, faithfully; it is reconciled here and now with personal action and human need. In contrast, on the negative side, pointlessness and ambiguity in prayer argue to an attitude of faithlessness; for here the petitioner is truly the child who cannot judge the paramount needs of the human community.

What must be prayed for today are the great social movements that have the character of rebirth within which men are striving for the dignity and purpose of manhood, that are leading us to the breach of catastrophe or hope. It is in these movements that the Spirit longs to exert a collective ministry, to give His mandate to the ideologies and enthusiasms which are so deeply human. Unity is the boundless desire of the Holy Spirit; it should also be the theme, object, and purpose of prayer.

Finally, by way of consequence, social action is the normal expression and fulfillment of the Christian community, at Mass, at the Sacraments, or at prayer. It is important to stress this because many Christians tend to see the prayer of the Church as an end in itself. But this thinking cannot represent the thought of Christ. His act of sacrifice is meant to form Christians capable of witnessing to Him through contact, engagement, and leadership, through lives which are deeply human and capable even of superhuman love.

Our own times offer us opportunity to reflect, by way of contrast, upon the pietism of our recent history, with its concentration upon the purely or selfishly personal and its implicit denial that man must live for all or deny all, or further, must abandon hope of being whole if he separates himself from the whole. History tells us that the pendulum of time is sweeping to extremes of subjectivism, to cults of selfishness and savage irresponsibility. We must bring it back to balance by taking up the burdens of mankind as our own, with an entirely new vision and confidence. And we must do this perhaps as a condition for continued existence itself.

Moreover, if we reflect on the nature of grace, we must admit that grace works to communicate itself in attitudes, and that it is efficient also in being directed to specific acts. By way of illustration, it has been said that the great dilemma of the religious person of our day is the conflict between rising public need and the progressive limitations of institutional life, which reduce drastically his possibilities of choice, and, in a manner of speaking, inhibit the full expression of divine life. This conflict also touches the layman, whose presence to society requires a freedom of movement in which he can sow what God has given him, so that the Divine Reaper may harvest when He chooses.

In the same vein, distracting and sometimes irrelevant discussions about the "emerging layman," and later, the "submerging layman," often miss the point of both Christian witness and of grace itself. The layman will never become what he really is, will never sufficiently learn and exercise his mission, until the Church knows him for what he is and trusts him in the field. In a parallel way, it is quite useless, at the present stage of civil rights, to tell the Negro that he must lift himself up through education and hard work; that he must exploit present opportunities. It is also very nearly useless to tell the layman that he must rise, that he must make himself heard, that he must make of his milieu an arena of Christian influence. The neglected point is this; both the Negro and the layman (if we may continue to use the example) have responded up to now to that measure of freedom given them by society or by the Church. In both cases, their record of response has been heroic; the Negro's in what he has done to build this country, and in what he is doing to purify it of its divisions and hatreds; the layman in a comparable pioneer role in the institutional rise of the Church, and in his loyalty to the substance of Catholicism. But, practically speaking, neither can be expected to do more in society or in the Church until more freedom is granted them, until their respective citizenship has been secured, until the implications of their presence in society and in the Church is recognized and dealt with. The only Negroes, in a negative, submerged sense, are those who still think of themselves as Negroes; the only laymen are those who think of themselves as laymen, in the merely permissive sense which still has such force. Perhaps the terms "human being" and "Christian" are respectively closer to the reality of both. Yet it is a sobering fact that neither Negro nor layman can think of himself in terms that express his dignity, as long as society or the Church neglect to do so.

Recently, an American cartoonist was given recognition for his original treatment of an important theme. In his cartoon, a brutish type of prehistoric man, club in hand, dumbly watches an astronaut's space capsule wheel through the sky above him. The prehistoric man is captioned "Human Relations." The cartoon invites our thoughtful reflection. It is the task of the Christian today to discover why science has left our sense of the human out of its account; why "isms" so occupy human consciousness; why men are quick to speak and loath to listen; why compassion is so rare; why tension and unhappiness are so common; why reality is so often avoided in favor of escapism; why moral sense is often reduced to selfish or group interest; why violence and mass murder are shrugged aside; why men turn to their weapons more unhesitantly than ever before; why men who are in fact brothers yet live as strangers; why some men love Christ yet hate His brothers; why, on the other hand, some reject Christ yet love His brothers; why so many respectable Christians are, in Samuel Butler's words, "equally horrified to hear the Christian religion doubted or to see it practiced."

Do we admit the stubborn truth behind Léon Bloy's warning: "The worst evil lies not in committing crimes, but in neglecting the good we can do"? Are we aware that every quality of mind and body, every resource of parentage and education, every influence of friendship, circumstance and grace, have come to us from God for reinvestment in other lives? Pius XII has said: "More and more the weight of the whole Church rests on the shoulders of each Catholic." And he relates these words to the layman in this fashion: "The consecration of the world is essentially the work of the laymen themselves, of men who are intimately a part of economic and social life. . . . May the layman be entrusted with tasks that he can fulfill as well or even better than the priest, and may he, under the limits of his function . . . be able to act freely and exercise his responsibility." Pope Paul has expressed the same paternal concern: "It is necessary to remake Christian society; it is necessary to awaken it, to be aware that we are responsible! This is a tremendous word, dynamic, unsettling, and energetic. He who understands (it) can no longer remain sleeping and indifferent. . . . We are responsible for our times, for the life of our brothers and we are responsible before our Christian conscience. . . . Now is the hour, the hour of the laity. It is the hour of souls, those who have understood that to be a Christian involves a commitment, since they can take part directly in this ministry of salvation, but they also assume a great burden, a risk and a duty."

Albert Camus has neatly and powerfully summed up our present state, against which we must react with the same fear so often reserved for commitment:

Today freedom has not many allies. I have been known to say that the real passion of the twentieth century is slavery. That was a bitter remark which did an injustice to all those men whose sacrifice and example every day help us to live. But I merely wanted to express that anguish I feel every day when faced with the decrease of liberal energies, the prostituting of words, the slandered victims, the justification of oppression, the insane admiration of force.

We see a multiplication of those minds of whom it has been said that they seemed to count an inclination toward slavery as an ingredient of virtue. We see the intelligence seeking justifications for its fear, and finding them readily, for every cowardice has its own philosophy. Indignation is measured, silences take counsel from one another, and history has ceased to be anything but Noah's cloak that is spread over the victim's obscenity.

In short, all flee real responsibility, the effort of being consistent or of having an opinion of one's own, in order to take refuge in the parties or groups that will think for them, express their anger for them, and make their plans for them. Contemporary intelligence seems to measure the truth of doctrines and causes solely by the number of armored divisions that each can put into the field.*

It remains for us to dare to seek out and to master the many faces of Christian charity. We must have the audacity to witness to the Life that is Jesus Christ, and in the process really to live. Love alone is redemptive, works for a common language, engenders mutual sincerity, brings about mutual confidence, puts men on a course which bypasses the pits of ruin to build bridges of trust and unity in the human community. "The greatness of an enterprise," wrote Saint-Exupéry, "is before all else, to unite men. There is only one true luxury, and that is the luxury of human relations."

Love banishes fear. It banishes the fear of striking out alone, fear of the inert and satisfied majority, fear of ideas and struggle and thankless engagement, fear of Christ and of what

* Albert Camus, *Resistance, Rebellion and Death* (New York: Alfred A. Knopf, 1961), pp. 100-101.

He might ask, fear of the brother and what he might need, fear of life and fear of death. Let the witness dare to express and live the sentiments of Archbishop Helden Camara as he accepted his See of Recife in Brazil:

Let no one be surprised at seeing me in the company of persons reputed to be persuasive and dangerous, leftists or rightists, of the majority or of the opposition, reformists or anti-reformists, anti-revolutionaries or revolutionaries, men of good faith or of faithlessness. Let no one try to bind me to a group, tie me to a party, have me make friends with their friends and adopt their enmities . . . We cannot afford to relinquish banners which are right, merely because they have been carried by the wrong hands. How can we fear movements that are deeply Christian in essence?

"If God is for us, who is against us? He that spared not even His own Son, but delivered Him us for us all, how has he not also with Him, given us all things? . . . Who then shall separate us from the love of Christ: Shall tribulation? Or distress? Or famine? Or nakedness? Or danger? Or persecution? Or the sword? . . . But in all these things, we overcome, because of Him that has loved us." (Romans 8, 32, 35, 37.)*

* Archbishop Helder Camara, quoted in *America*, May 2, 1964, p. 590.

2. Christ and the Shape of Mankind

A dangerous incomprehension, an unhealthy pessimism, and even in some quarters a quiet, unformulated panic mark the Christian approach to mankind today. Strangers to the world that we are expected to redeem, we look about us "unknowing and unwinking," out of our depth and element as perhaps never before in history. On an alarming scale, we live in the present with the least worldly contact possible, while the future has lost its promise of exhilaration and opportunity. What masses on our horizon is a series of threats: the continued expansion of Communism, the loss to the Church of Latin America, social discorder and bloodshed over civil rights, the arms escalation toward World War III, the collapse of white supremacy and the "Western way of life." Yet, in regard to personal change—the purification and development required of Christians by the stress of these issues, and the human and courageous reply that suggests concern and willingness—we are found ignorant and afraid. Whether unconsciously or knowingly, we have taken precise and effective pains to keep the agony of mankind remote from us; we have little desire to understand it and even less to share it. Given such attitudes, the Christian's relapse into passivity, shallowness, and resentment is inevitable.

We see the Church, like a new Jewish Diaspora, reduced to beleaguered outposts in Christian countries, or thrust progressively into a minority position by the biological eruption of the non-Christian world. We see that awesome phenomenon, a positive science which, while lavishing on mankind a breathtaking variety of materiality, takes its toll of the human spirit, dulling our human sympathies and outdistancing our moral capability to use it wisely. We view Communism with terror and with an unresolved guilt complex, since its secularism is more logical and unfettered than the practical Godlessness that the West has chosen. And we wonder, with something like despair, if we have the vitality to regain that supremely Christian quality which is the historic mark of its being, the equality between principle and action.

We see the headlong struggle of the people of Africa and of the East for their share of creation, for those things that will make life more livable and the possession of truth more possible are in our consciousness. We see new tools of secular redemption on every side, many of them unfamiliar to us, many of them designed exactly to serve man in this world. Having all this in sight before us, with a superficiality of judgment unworthy of us as Christians, we begin almost instinctively the long and joyless retreat to conservative ramparts. As Fr. Albert Dondeyne has observed: "The current Christian is a conservative by vocation . . . his belief in God leading either to a dogmatic intolerance or a conservative fixation, or an ethic of resignation and inaction." With growing alarm, we sense ourselves as members of an ingrown society, whose right to existence and voice is either challenged or bluntly ignored. And our response varies from a mass inferiority complex to a progressive loss of faith in the God of history and in the world of man.

Meanwhile, in a body which is meant by nature to be expansive and catalytic, retreat into the corporate self goes on. Imperceptible assaults of fear obscure the meaning and demands of life, and the trivial increasingly occupies the Christian consciousness. Christianity in these days moves in a new costume. It is no longer the cult of the valiant, no longer the creed of religious entrepreneurs who feared only "him who is able to destroy both soul and body in hell" (St. Matthew 10:28). The transcendent intelligence and social virility that were an irresistible credential of our religion in its best days have been adulterated to an effeminacy and childishness dedicated to solidifying themselves in the security of a perennial adolescence. We are marked by the territorial jealousy of the well-to-do son, who in the shadow of his mother, defends his possessions from the aggressive envy of the poor and the ostracized. And the shadow that we flee into is one of social position and institutional security, while a curious equivocation of speech comes into practice, a rewriting of dogma in order that the faith may justify personal sterility, a harmonizing of morality until it becomes a vehicle of convenience. As Emmanuel Mounier contends: "More often than one likes to admit one meets under the name of Christianity a code of moral and religious propriety whose chief concern seems to be to discourage outbursts of feeling, to fill up all chasms, to apologize for audacity, to do away with suffering, to bring down the appeals of the Infinite to the level of domestic conversation, and to tame the anguish of our state."* Such a disguise has introduced its own attrition into history and into contemporary society. Richard Cardinal Cushing, in a Pastoral Letter, wrote: "Christ's members are on the defensive in most places, in decline in some, on the upgrade in only a few. Christianity, once the center of gravity of our civilization, is today a peripheral activity. At work, in leisure, in political, social, sexual, educational, professional, and family interests, the mass of the modern community is almost without trace of Christian values."

Our present sensibility is a measure of what we have made of the transcendent Catholic who is Christ Our Lord. We espouse our own heresies these days, they are still Christological in nature, they are still a misconception of Him Who is

* *Crosscurrents.*

truth itself. In the lives of many Catholics, one notices a distortion of sacred reality, an image of the Saviour whose dimensions are our own limitations, produced by our imperception and cowardice. Humanized and domesticated, our Christ is the projection of ourselves; the feminine, adult figure, whose heart and arms invite us to a love which demands no return; the "Friend" in the tabernacle Who, isolated from human life and attention, waits upon recognition from men. According to the gospel of our illusion, Christ becomes the Great Advocate of childishness, the Great Sanctuary from the harsh world and the intolerable neighbor, the Great Pleader for understanding and company: "Unless you become as little children"; "Come to Me all you who labor and are heavily burdened"; "He that comes to Me, I will not cast out." The words are taken out of context, and we refuse to balance the scales with what He said of love, of the Cross, of the hard and glorious task of learning Him and of living Him. His Person is made to fit the words, becoming a personification of an emasculated ideal, produced by false interpretations of the Gospel, the Codes of fearful men. The reality of the Son of God is diminished beyond recognition; He exists as the sanction of an aberrant self that rejects anything that threatens its safety or invites it into adult life.

What we have done to Christ is precisely what we have done to ourselves. "To be a man is a process of becoming man." Any compression of the distance between Christ and ourselves, any fabrication of Him as one of the herd, any destruction of the personal element of what "ought to be," is to attack our nature at its roots by insisting that it *is* rather than it is *becoming*. One cannot but conclude that one of the terrors that confronts our age is our concept of ourselves, our conviction of "having arrived," of having climbed to a plateau of conclusion that leaves little room for depth or expansion. Christ in His Incarnate Manhood grew in time, and He realized completion only in the supreme moments of His death, resurrection, and exaltation. It must be said therefore, that He was not living a mere ideal—He was living life as it must be lived, being human life itself. Shakespeare understood well this aspect of human nature: "It hath been taught us from the primal state, that he which is was wished until he were" (*Antony and Cleopatra* I, iv, 41-42). Any debasement of Christ then, or any assumption that we can manipulate Him into identification with our feeble likeness is to create inevitably the static negation that we have decided to be. It is to invite us to evade self-knowledge and maturation, to say "no" to life itself, on the premise that we know what we need to know of ourselves, and that we are everything that we can be.

By a consequent logic, following abruptly upon such an affirmation of self, mankind becomes an enemy because it can neither accept our image nor can it be indifferent to it. We have concluded, in the most opaque and egotistical fashion, that humanity is what we are, that it is as satisfied, as desirous of stability, as it is socially immobile. But the reality is quite different from our view; it rather speaks of explosive growth in birth, of progress in technology, of struggle for antonomy and dignity. Moreover, by the very nature of their vigorous search for truth and social condition, most men cannot be other than demanding of our time, our knowledge, our energies and humanitarianism; nor can they help but be critical of our failure in response. In reality, the whole race is being forced to face itself through ideology, through events, through communications, through social revolution; the minority, through the social dislocation born of the distress of the majority; the majority, through the irresistible momentum of its own social emergence. In truth, we must abandon the debate that we are striving for a static condition which is our version of peace. Peace rather, if it is to be won, will appear as a controlled and ordered revolution, in which our values will direct the currents of our times in such a way that all men will be saved from utter destruction or general social collapse; saved indeed for themselves and for Christ.

II

An analysis of the Christ of modern Christians, His features, His speech, His asceticism, His life, would possibly invite us to consider the following historical events. First Luther and the Reformers carried the diminished Renaissance Christian message to its fateful extreme, bringing the unkillable, uninstructed, and undisciplined hope of reform into open revolt. Then Christian suspicion of scientific efforts from Galileo's time not only allowed materialism to take root in the dark corners of society but gave creation and its processes over to materialistic scientism for a psuedo-redemption. In time, national revolutions toppled the old orders in France, Italy, and Germany. Almost invariably, these changes occurred over the protest of the Church and without the involvement of Catholics. In the midst of a process which was at least potentially Christian, Catholics severely anathematized and were fearful and silent. And because Catholics were absent or actively in opposition to the hopes of man, it was inevitable that the revolutions took on a bitterly anti-Catholic character; and that the creation of modern man, industrialized and politically emancipated, occurred at a distance from believers and apart from the Church. This is the tragedy of which Pius XI was to speak with so bitter an insight.

Now Communism is upon us, the most vicious, relentless, and messianic of all the "isms" of history; and we fail quite generally to see that our stubbornly cherished secularism, our flight from the issues of time and human predicament is its secret, powerful, and unacknowledged ally. We fail to see that its assertion, "The achievements of the kingdoms of this world is man's most important issue," sounds with logic and lucidity in the vacuum left by tired Christian energies, gospel lip service, and pharisaic moralism. We may attempt to forestall its massive onrush by pouring extensive economic, material, technical, political, and military aid into the underdeveloped areas of the world, but perhaps our money has failed to substitute for our presence, our intelligent and selfless service. "Every neglected poor man is a source of terror, his wounds can turn to weapons overnight." Moreover, to offer a philosophy which expresses itself only in technical and material things is already to have capitulated to the Communists. Charles Malik wrote:

> For the Communists mean these things *and something more.* They provide ideas about life and destiny and government and history; they are not afraid of coming to these old societies and telling them: this is rotten, and that is rotten, and you must understand and interpret yourselves completely differently . . . There is nothing that man rejects with greater horror than a meaningless existence, and if all your technical and material assistance only manages to leave his existence meaningless, he will suspect that your existence is meaningless or that you are keeping its meaning from him; and in either case, he will end by hating you.*

III

Historic Christianity teaches that the Incarnation of the Son of God is the great axis that divides time into two periods: one of long preparation, the other a period of progressive development in Christ. In the earliest Christian preaching, these were the classical divisions of history (Acts 17:30), and by the gift of God and the choice of His Providence, we are partners to the second phase. We are presently tending toward that sublime moment when "all things are made subject

* Charles Malik, quoted in *World Campus,* October, 1961.

to him, then the Son himself will also be made subject to him who subjected all things to him, that God may be all in all" (I Corinthians 15:28). The Incarnation then is the central historic moment of the universe, of time, and of man. Everything finds its reason in the Word Made Flesh, everything converges toward Him. He is the "firstborn" and the Head of all creation. Teilhard de Chardin wrote:

> Over the centuries an all-embracing plan seems in truth to be unfolding around us. Something is afoot in the universe, some issue is at stake, which cannot be better described than a process of gestation and birth; the birth of the spiritual reality formed by the souls of men and by the matter which they bear along with them. Laboriously, through the medium and by virtue of human activity, the new earth is gathering its forces, emerging and purifying itself. No, we are not like the blooms in a bunch of flowers, but rather the leaves and blossoms of some great tree on which all things appear in due season and due place, in time with and at the behest of the All.*

The Church of Paul, the Fathers, and the Christian Middle Ages had a far more profound idea of these things than we do; she did not hesitate to explore boldly the implication of Christ's advent in the world that He had created, and His identification with us in human flesh. From a speculation that was Christocentric came an understanding and a realization that made preaching relevant and full-bodied and humanistic. For these earlier Christians, the universe was gathered into its microcosm man, through whom it reached identity, purpose, and destiny. Man not only embodied the vast spectrum of life, being a composite of the elements of the universe, he contained the cosmos within himself by his spiritual grasp of

* Pierre Teilhard de Chardin, *The Meaning and Constructive Value of Suffering, Jubilee,* June, 1962, Vol. 10, No. 2, translated by Noel Lindsay.

it, by his intellectual assertion of its nature. Today it is a rare experience to find a contemporary Christian writer who will see the pertinence of a cosmology of the Gospels.

> We are subtly invited to flee from a world to which we have not found the key into the inner deserts of a spirituality exasperated to complete withdrawal. . . . This Christianity, ready to abandon the earth to its Apocalypse, ready to fly to an invisible Church, ready to desert the Body of Christ, to this Christianity we shall never cease proclaiming the meaning of earth, of duty, of history which all together —breathe the word with all its fragrance of the soil—make up the modern meaning of humanity.*

And as crown of this profound comprehension of the universe, and at the same time its fundamental basis, stood the truth that was Christ, the Revelation of God by the Son of God. "He is the image of the invisible God, the firstborn of every creature. For in him were created all things in the heavens and on the earth, things visible and things invisible, whether Thrones, or Dominations, or Principalities, or Powers. All things have been created through and unto him, and he is before all creatures, and in him all things hold together" (Colossians 1:15-17). In the Incarnation, the Word of God becomes personally man; the man Christ becomes personally God. In consequence, Christ is God in a human way; Christ is man in a divine way. St. Thomas says that in Our Lord human nature is taken up that it might be the Person of the Son of God—that in Christ nature might experience the messianic and redemptive encounter with God. In the same manner the universe finds entrance and return to its maker in Christ, and in those who operate in His Name.

Our Lord then, as the Word, is the Architect of the uni-

* Emmanuel Mounier, *Be Not Afraid* (New York: Sheed & Ward, 1962), p. 105.

verse—He is the Divine Thought Who brought into existence
the vast and complex variety of life. "All things were made
through him and without him was made nothing that has been
made" (John 1:3). But in regard to all creatures His more
than this; to the Seraphim and the choirs of angels, to every
man born into this world, to all sensitive and vegetative life
down to the most insignificant one-celled being, to rocks and
minerals and metals, to all these He is the central point and
focus, the center about which all being revolves, the tendency
and attractive force toward Whom all things are drawn. The
cycle of existence began with Him, and within all natures lie
the potent seeds of return, first to Him and through Him to
the Father. The Redemption, therefore, is the first stage in a
return interrupted by sin, and at the same time an assured
fact and a final accomplishment. "And I, if I be lifted up from
the earth, will draw all things to myself" (John 12:32).

"I went into the Higher part of myself, and higher still I
found the Kingdom of the Word. Impelled by curiosity to
explore still further, I descended deep into myself, and yet I
found Him deeper still. I looked outside and met Him far
beyond everything exterior to me. I looked within; He is
more inward than myself. And I recognized the truth of what
I had read, that we live and move and have our being in
Him." St. Bernard knew that man has definition and identity
only in Christ, that the human person is finally known by the
grace of Christ within him—that Christ is in man as a second
self and that there is an identity between himself and Christ in
nature and in Spirit. As Gabriel Marcel so acutely remarks:
"There is no unique subject; no personality without otherness; no consciousness turned in upon itself; no real being
without intersubjectivity." And no man without Christ. His
Redemption, incessantly at work within us, is the assumption
of our manhood into His, that we might become heirs and
brothers and sons of the Father. He Who is Being "has the

countenance of a Person, and He has chosen to identify Himself with the imperfect persons that we are. "Abide in me," He said, "and I in you" (John 15:4).

So Our Lord effected our Redemption by living the human course and by dying to everything murderous and divisive in our nature. In the Resurrection, He universalized His Life, making it common and catholic, injecting into the veins of our humanity His own union with the Divinity, givng Himself over to us as a Legacy and as a general Property. He was now for us Way, Truth, Life, Decency and Dignity—Salvation and Eternal Union. He had redeemed us all, the one race in many persons—through Him, redemption is an incontrovertible fact of human existence. And all of this with but one condition, that we agree to our redemption, that we make our fiat to His Life which is now ours; and that, in fidelity, we insist on nothing less than this, but rather the "more" of finding Him anew and agreeing once again.

To help us assent, He gave us the pattern of a life, the only one worth living, which ranged from Bethlehem to the Garden of his victory; and the sublime majesty of that Life has entered into and conquered time to the extent that He is as relevant to modern man as He was to the poor peasants of Galilee. An invitation comes to every man and He awaits a response. "You have not chosen me, but I have chosen you" (John 15:16). "Again he sent out other servants, saying, 'Tell those who are invited . . . everything is ready; come to the marriage feast'" (St. Matthew 22:4). "A man had two sons; and he came to the first and said, 'Son, go and work today in my vineyard'" (St. Matthew 21:28). "But Peter answered him and said, 'Lord, if it is thou, bid me come to thee over the water.' And he said, 'Come'" (St. Matthew 14:28). "He who is not with me is against me, and he who does not gather with me, scatters" (St. Matthew 12:30). "He who has ears to hear, let him hear" (St. Matthew 13:9).

But the invitation soon involves a command of renunciation. "If anyone wishes to come after me, let him deny himself, and take up his cross, and follow me" (St. Matthew 16:24). "Take my yoke upon you, and learn from me, for I am meek and humble of heart; and you will find rest to your souls" (St. Matthew 11:29). "Amen, amen, I say to you, unless the grain of wheat falls into the ground and dies, it remains alone. But if it dies, it brings forth much fruit" (John 12:24). "For if you love those that love you, what reward shall you have? Do not even the publicans do that?" (St. Matthew 5:46). "This is my commandment, that you love one another as I have loved you" (John 15:12). "Amen, amen, I say to you, no servant is greater than his master, nor one who is sent greater than he who sent him" (John 13:16).

Renunciation causes resemblance, which grows to union with Him. "In that day you will know that I am in my Father, and you in me, and I in you" (John 14:20). "If anyone love me, he will keep my word, and my Father will love him, and we will come to him and make our abode with him" (John 14:23). "He who sees me sees also the Father" (John 14:9). "He who abides in me, and I in him, he bears much fruit; for without me you can do nothing" (John 15:5). "That all may be one, even as thou, Father, in me and I in thee; that they also may be one in us" (John 17:21). The personality of Christ cuts through the complexities of modern life, pierces the barricades of delusion and vanity, conquers the affectations of men, renews the humdrum and boredom of existence with a fresh and organic power. "You are already clean because of the word that I have spoken to you (John 15:3). It matters little that we are weak and sinful, vacillating and treacherous, "competing with one another in guarding ourselves against Him," as Yves Congar says. We are His by creation and conquest, and what He did for us once the Church continues to do with the same solicitude and sovereign power.

IV

It is undoubtedly the responsibility of those within the Church to announce the Christ of history to the men of their time, which is another way of saying that we must tell man about himself, about his meaning and his purpose. As Henri Delubac wrote:

> Even in these times of intoxication mingled with anxiety, amidst the most pressing necessities, it is the role of the Christian . . . to raise his voice and remind those who forget it of their own nobility; man is only himself, he only exists for himself here and now if he can discover within himself, in silence, some untouched region, some mysterious background which, whether gloomy or cheerful, commonplace or tragic, is not encroached upon by the cares of the present. To seek to give him back an understanding of this is not to plunge him in the waters of Lethe, to stupefy him with opium, or to give him Dutch courage. And to call back to the duties of the day one who lives entirely in a future which he sees rising out of his own creative energy is by no means to try to snatch from him his faith in man. On the contrary, it is to make him have a respect for man wherever he is found. It is to forbid his ever making use of the man of today as a mere instrument for the purposes of the man of tomorrow. Above all, it is to prevent him, both now or in the future, whether rich or poor, successful or unsuccessful, from being entirely absent, completely estranged from himself.*

All of this is, in reality, to recast the problems of our own age in terms which are at once more radically valid and less immediate than those of diplomacy, sociology, or natural science. It is unquestionable that the sciences and other modes of

* Henri De Lubac, *Catholicism* (New York: Sheed & Ward, 1958), pp. 198-99.

thought are valid in themselves, but they necessarily imply a limitation of concept, terminology, and action. They deal with the possible in the political order; they tell us what social relationships are at the present time, or they search the world of matter. They can deal adequately with aspects of being, or say something about its appearances and manifestations, but they cannot announce the inner substance of history or point the direction of its term. Only Christians can do this. The relationship of man to Christ must therefore be dramatized before the world by fervent, intelligent believers, who are men of their times, skilled in their vocation within the Church, men who live habitually and instinctively according to the mind of Christ. Such Christians are, by definition, mediators between their Lord and their world, a world which will fulfill itself only in Him, through a continuing Christian Incarnation. Failing in this effort, creation becomes a source of suspicion and scandal to the introverted believer; it tends to remain inert and incomplete, incapable of growing or offering material for human growth. And in time, as history continues to show us, creation passes over to other more skilled and dedicated hands than ours.

Another aspect of the relationship between the living Christ and the believer reminds us that we attain unity with Our Lord through unity with one another. In fact it is impossible for men to order or to rule the organic world unless they rule the world of persons by service. He who neither knows nor serves his neighbor is a dangerous man with the things of nature. In these terms, therefore, the impersonalism of Western man is not only the measure of the loss of Christ through the loss of one another, it is the source of our hesitancy and fear with which we regard the works of our hands. There are, for example, not many of us who do not recognize the bomb as a harbinger of man-made eschatology.

Aldous Huxley has summarized our position with a great measure of precision and power:

> We began by lacking charity towards nature, so that instead of trying to cooperate with . . . the Logos on the inanimate and sub-human levels, we try to dominate and exploit, we waste the earth's mineral resources, ruin its soil, ravage its forests, pour filth into its rivers and poisonous fumes into its air. From lovelessness in relation to Nature we advance to lovelessness in relation to art—a lovelessness so extreme that we have effectively killed all the fundamental or useful arts and set up various kinds of mass-production by machines in their place. And, of course, this lovelessness in regard to art is at the same time a lovelessness in regard to the human beings who have to perform the fool-proof and grace-proof tasks imposed by our mechanical art-surrogates and by the interminable paper work connected with mass-production and mass-distribution.*

Men live today in the shadow of mischance, haunted by the dread of atomic miscalculation. And Catholics, quite generally, are allowing the questions of peace and conscience and nuclear development to be bypassed, or to be discussed by others. If not this, when they do speak, they revert commonly to historic formulas or major premises about a just war whose relevance to our stalemate is at best questionable. It would seem that, on this score alone, contemporary events are forcing all men into a corner. As the question of atomic annihilation mushrooms in our consciousness, as we face the "have not" peoples of the world, as we assess the meaning of "color," as we strive to discover the meaning of Christianity in face of Christian division and competition—all related issues—the implications of Christ in His universe grow not only clearer

* Aldous Huxley, *The Perennial Philosophy* (New York: Harper & Row, 1945), pp. 93-94.

but more exigent every hour. Events are making Christians the keepers of their brothers in an altogether new way; the keepers of their minds and hearts, the guardians of their sense of history, the stewards of the souls of men. They alone can grasp, and help others to grasp this link between men and the Father that is Christ's Body, Which is at once the Saviour and them.

To the perceptive, the choices thrust upon us by our age are, in fact, similar in many respects to the hard decisions imposed by God upon ancient Israel. Upon Jewish adherence to Him depended their continuance as a people—to the Jew, life by the covenant meant personal realization and the guarantee of a share in God's promise. "And you shall dwell in the land which I gave to your fathers, and you shall be my people, and I will be your God" (Ezekiel 36:28). The covenant made by Christ with us in His Church is even more graphic in its demands; and Christian history, up to our own day, continues to spell out the price demanded of those who would live and act in fidelity to Christ's Body.

The charity demanded by human unity, "when thou shalt see one naked, cover him, and despise not thy own flesh" (Isaias 58:7), is now a deeper need than ever; on its acceptance hinges the divine judgment, a judgment already implicit in our refusal or acceptance of man. " 'Lord, when did we see thee hungry, or thirsty, or a stranger, or naked, or sick, or in prison, and did not minister to thee?' . . . 'Amen I say to you, as long as you did not do it for one of these least ones, you did not do it for me' " (St. Matthew 25:44-45).

The hopes of man, as Christian minds from Paul to Teilhard de Chardin agree, come to their summit and to their unity in Christ. The possibility for general disarmament, the chances for a peaceful reduction of Communist inflence and geographical control, the acceptance of the emerging peoples into the hegemony of nations, progress toward international and world government, the checking of family instability and breakup, even the hopes and accomplishments of the Ecumenical Council—in the final analysis, all of these depend in a general way upon the believer's understanding of Christ as a personal and cosmic reality.

Such an assertion is not offered as an exercise in the simplicism that tosses both sacral and profane into a mental void, where nothing can be seen and dealt with in itself. The statement rather suggests that the Incarnation is a truth at once general and particular, looming so large in the human mind that all history must take it into account, consciously or no. It is at once a sacred center of faith, a nucleus of intellectual resonance, a coloration of mind, a way of regarding the world. And among believers it is perennially clear that historic events act as a ferment of faith vindicating and even developing dogma, in the sense that events are requiring a fundamental, mature tide of intelligence and liberality as the condition of man's efforts to create his world community and to make it habitable by men.

Under such pressures Christian life today is being painfully broken and recast. Its new shape is that of historic openness, of reverence before events, which simultaneously suggest preponderant movements and the course of Christian purification. Christians are called to the tasks of adults within the body of mankind:

> Our desire is to work for the good of the world, in its interests and for its salvation. We believe that the salvation we offer is necessary for it. This affirmation implies many others. It implies that we look upon the world with immense sympathy. If the world thinks itself to be a stranger from Christianity, Christianity does not consider itself a stranger from the world, no matter what attitude the world adopts towards it. Let the world know that the representa-

tive and promoter of the Christian religion esteems and
loves it with a great and inexhaustible love. It is the love
which our faith plants in the heart of the Church, whose
only purpose is to serve as a channel for the vast and won-
derful love of God for men. This means that the mission of
Christianity is one of friendship in the midst of mankind, a
mission of understanding, encouragement, advancement,
elevation, and—we say it again—of salvation.*

* Pope Paul VI at Bethlehem.

3. With My Body, I Worship You

"He that has a wife and children has given hostages to fortune; for they are impediments to great enterprise, either of virtue or mischief." Bacon's observation on marriage can be thought cynical or amusing, yet it has serious overtones for married people. It is the rare partner to a marriage who does not sometimes reflect on the boredom, the human loss and the harsh responsibilities that follow a lifetime involvement with another person. If the union is approached in a highly moral sense, baffling questions frequently arise. Where is the mutual insight and union of will that the sacrament is said to cause? Where is the mystical oneness idealized by St. Augustine: "The Church, living with Christ, Who lives forever, may never be divorced from Him." Where is the mutual liberality resting upon Christ's immolation for His Church? Where is the life-giving expansion into society implied by the relationship of one community to another? And if the marriage is viewed less realistically, the questions arise on a lower plane, but with greater insistence. Who is this stranger? How could I have made this mistake? How faithful is he? On this level, the expectation of happiness may be as unrealistic as the education for marriage was limited. The reactions, therefore, are predictable; the best of them is stoicism, the worst, alienation and separation.

Yet this much is certain, a marriage without questions does not exist, for the couple are living out a mystery in their lives. And living out a mystery means a practical familiarity with puzzlement and suffering. "Christ represented marriage

49

through His Passion," says Pius XII. He took His Church as Spouse only through the shedding of blood. And married people who think that they can possess each other without experiencing pain have a tenuous hold on reality.

Moreover, the modern marriage is increasingly exposed to social change, because the world today is characterized by a quality of modification which is complex and steadily increasing in tempo. Under these conditions, the institution of marriage is more and more vulnerable. Here, as in other social groupings, a vicious circle is operating. The modern community, constantly shifting in its elements and values, draws heavily from the family, but does not adequately support it. Society contributes little stability to the family through law; it gives the large family neither sufficient approval nor financial support; it provides only marginal education for marriage, acting as though this is a strict prerogative of the Church. The family, in turn, left to resources unequal for its preservation, casts its instability upon society through a shifting of its own responsibility.

As a result, some see the family declining as an institution. The United States, Britain, and West Germany, it is said, are well on the way to becoming welfare states of the Scandinavian type. So profound is this quiet falling apart that the family will soon have little more status than a social one, becoming something of a sociological convenience where ties of blood mean little more than the impersonal relationships of a boardinghouse. Others, less pessimistic, still point to the annual wreckage of some 400,000 American marriages; to the stopgap measures of government in the form of family aid; to the growing inability of the American male to meet the tests of husband and father, and to the logical complement of such a leadership vacuum, in the unhealthy aggressiveness of the wife and mother; to the alarming lack of communication between parents and children; to the tendency to tear sex from its moral fabric and to equate it with love; to the absence within families of a sense of belonging to a larger whole—to community, nation, mankind, Church.

If solutions are suggested, it seems that they must begin at this precise point—with the education of the person to acceptance, first of himself and then, through a strong sense of self-possession, of others. In a realistic sense, the self-donation demanded by marriage is quite impossible in a person who knows nothing of self-mastery and self-direction; in a word, of maturity.

"The body is an obstacle as well as a help; a limitation as much as a means, a burden that often oppresses the soul." So Jean Mouroux begins his lucid treatment of the cleavage of body and soul; so too must begin any fundamental consideration of the problem of modern marriage. Self-acceptance implies acceptance of the body; but the body is gross, importunate, rebellious; the soul is languid, obscure, and digressive. The two appear cast off from each other's presence, unwilling partners to a union, each with its own object and purpose, each responding to the needs of the other only with reluctance. The body, one with the soul in human existence, resists subjection to it and would reduce the primacy of spirit to a mere animation, working to make its animality the strongest voice in man. For its own part, the soul feels itself enervated, turbid, confused by the claims of the body, slow to command and weak to police. Body and spirit are at war, not only because of sin, but because they are body and spirit. So union of the two exists, but what a union! tense, divisive, fragile, an association of dependence, but more often, a complex, brutal struggle.

Moreover, as if it were not enough that the battle is drawn on issues of matter and spirit, on the conflict between appetite and the insatiable human hunger for God, the battle is also drawn within the spirit itself and on purely spiritual grounds.

The soul does not know itself, it knows only an inner division —egoism and generosity, pride and truth, love and retreat. Its dark acts often reveal a complicity with the body; but often, too, it acts independently and by a pure spiritual initiative becomes both seeker and sought, instrument and goal, contradicting what it is by what it does. "You shall be as gods, knowing good and evil" (Genesis 3:5). "For I do not the good that I wish, but the evil that I do not wish, that I perform" (Romans 7:19). In most men, the law of Adam takes two general forms: The soul languishes under its carnality or, having attained a tenuous freedom from the flesh, it seeks new conquests for itself, new subjections to reassure its vanity. "We will magnify our tongue; our lips are our own; who is Lord over us?" (Psalm 11, 5).

"Who will deliver me from the body of this death? The grace of God through Jesus Christ our Lord" (Romans 7:24-25). By its originating sin, the soul cut its ties of grace with God, and in the same act cut its ties of grace with the body. In the married state people attempt an impossible ideal unless they have a strong hold on all possible sources of unity, human and divine. How often, by way of contrast, when a marriage reaches a precarious state, is heard the terrible remark, "We must think of the children," implying, of course, that husband and wife are past thinking of each other. Or in an even worse turn is the couple with whom consideration for their family no longer bears weight. The crippling diet of illusion that has been brought into many marriages becomes poisonously active there, passing largely unnoticed—the imaginative soarings and emotive dreams of adolescence assert themselves and become the common label of the adult. John Updike's Rabbit Angstrom is typical enough today to be almost endemic.

In this connection, the words of Christ are powerfully precise: "When the strong man, fully armed, guards his courtyard, his property is undisturbed. But if a stronger than he attacks and overcomes him . . ." (St. Luke 11:21-22). The married are so often the target and prey of blind forces, so often conquered by their very rebellion, so often predictably erratic in their response to personality and circumstance. The strong man who guards their courtyard does not exist; the work of self-conquest is often not begun, or if it is it remains far from attained. For call it what you will—sense of identity, integrity, self-possession—the conquest we speak of means openness to God, to spouse, neighbor, world—it means that one's human powers are in a constant living rhythm of reception and response. This conquest is a free flow of life toward the other, a gift neither disfigured by subjectivism nor corrupted by egoism nor stagnated by indifference. And finally, this conquest is a sense of reality, which is according to Mounier, in *Character of Man*, "a desire to live with the world, not lost in it, nor merely parallel with it, but in a discipline of exchange and interpenetration which is ever expanding the personal richness of life."

II

It would not be exaggerating, perhaps, to maintain that people of the West often have a markedly inferior psychological preparation for the institution of marriage. In this, both Church and society are at fault. The Church is fast realizing, it seems, that a religion which attempts to promote Christian personalism through prohibitions, through a liturgy dominated by clerics, and through traditional rather than apostolic organizations, has failed to make people ready for people, for community, for world. What is true in the case of all believers is particularly true in the personal communion that lies at the heart of the marriage experience. And in its turn society may one day better understand that the dubious maze of values exhibited in public and private life, in law and government, in business and entertainment are the greatest threat to its own harmony and efficiency and, on the other hand, that moral integrity contributes as much to the common good as social concern contributes to the vitality of religion. To a distressing degree, the old American debate as to what is religious and what is secular seldom displays an understanding of either, and seldom avoids a fruitless impasse.

At any rate, the critical situation of marriage today suggests that both society and Church have failed to contribute adequately to the formation of truly masculine men and truly feminine women. Such men and women would offer one another, by the force of their choice, a security of love guaranteed by their masculinity and their femininity.

C. G. Jung's theory of compensation indicates in this regard that man and woman are much more complementary than opposed to each other. Moreover, his explanation of unconscious archetypes suggests forcefully that men are truly masculine because of their feminine archetypes, and that their manliness is valid only insofar as their unconscious image of woman is valid. Conversely, a woman possesses femininity because she has objectively valid masculine ideals buried in her psyche which she sees reflected in the "manliness" of the male. Erich Fromm offers this valuable insight on Jung's theory:

> Above the universal, existential need for union rises a more specific, biological one: the desire for union between the masculine and feminine poles. The idea of this polarization is most strikingly expressed in the myth that originally man and woman were one, that they were cut in half, and from then on each male has been seeking for the lost female part of himself in order to unite again with her . . . The meaning of the myth is clear enough. Sexual polarization leads man to seek union in a specific way, that of union with the

other sex. The polarity between the male and female principles exists also *within* each man and each woman. Just as
physiologically man and woman each have hormones of the
opposite sex, they are bisexual also in the psychological
sense. They carry in themselves the principle of receiving
and of penetrating, of matter and spirit. Man—and woman
—finds union within himself only in the union of his female
and his male polarity.*

These two sets of poles or qualities, both conscious and
unconscious, "speak" to each other as they meet in male and
female; their very nature is to seek communion. So it is that
people see themselves in the one they love; in fact, love becomes a search to possess the self in the other.

What is the grasp of sex that so many moderns establish in
their unconscious life? It is certainly the product of many
ideas, many experiences, many imaginings—so frequently
brutalized that the union of the sexual polarities in the unconscious proves to be quite rare. The formulation begins, one
would suppose, with the prevalent cultural image of "person," which stresses, for the most part, the sensual and the
concrete, the visible and the acceptable. Ancillary to the notion of person follows what manhood and womanhood is
thought to be, mere sexual variations of a vaguely superficial
idea of person. Consequently, and by way of example, a man
will build his archetype of woman on an unbalanced parental
relationship, and he will reinforce this unconscious distortion
through "realistic" literature and the cultural chaos of the
communications media. Here he encounters the cult of the
sensory, the fixation upon the body, the equivocal portrayal
of love as sex, and of sex as love. Instead of being appre-
hended as a composite of spiritual, psychological, emotional,

* Erich Fromm, *The Art of Loving* (New York: Harper & Row, 1956),
p. 27.

and physical humanity, woman is misconceived as a "body," whose sex is the primary aspect of her being, whose purpose is exploitation as a sexual object.

It is this type, this woman, which the conscious has to deal with in its unconscious companion, which disgorges its image to conscious surface to pander to the person and to distract him, to spur his imagination to wanderings of fantastic unreality, to dull his hold upon reality by controlling attention.

Such unconscious fixation sends its shoots up into conscious life, where its corrupt influence is pervasive. Very often it can actually dominate and rule the conscious life. It is like a mysterious impurity of the blood, which flourishes unknown until it appears in nodules and eruptions upon the skin. Indulgent, bent upon governing consciousness and affectivity, the sick unconscious gradually and inexorably creates a hypereroticism, which manifests itself in some as narcissism, in others as egotism. Through unconscious determinance, the whole craving of man is absorbed in self-love, commonly manifesting itself in a love of sexual gratification or a love of self at the expense of the other.

Those in whom the aberration takes the form of narcissism are known for a degree of conscious sleepwalking—they move in something like an artificial twilight; their minds perceiving dull glimmerings of reality; their will moving in an ever-narrowing area of choice. Life for them can become a dream in which any thought can be thought, any circumstance can be possible or even probable. The realities of time and space are kept at distance, for they are profoundly boring or painful. Imagination controls the field of consciousness, spinning its illusions from memories, experiences, and vagaries in which the heroic self dominates and expands. Other people are ideal because they pay homage, or they are fixtures to be subdued. Meanwhile, the great coordinator of them all is the consciousness of a dreamer.

The other form of self-love seems to create the ruthless "practical" activist, whose illusory love is really an imperceptible growth in hate, in which the person deals with himself and others in wariness and anxiety, in peevish irascibility, waiting to assert a mastery, which in the real sense, is only another defeat. Stekel says well that this type of illusory love "is generally due to resentment. It always manifests an antagonistic attitude toward certain persons . . . It does not serve to appease one's need for love, but to hurt someone, to avoid defeat, or to procure an easy triumph for one's self."*

Looking at the personal and social roots of the subconscious of modern man, one is struck by the lack of emotional training offered by our education. Our society is sensate in nature, as psychologists point out; its rewards are almost invariably those of personal comfort, distraction, and security. Yet the efforts necessary to understand emotional life, as an ingredient of human life, are rather rare. Training in emotional discipline is even rarer. Yet when one thinks of the profound influence, for good or ill, which the emotions exert on human life, the need to understand the emotions for the purpose of integrating their drives into a fully human potential becomes urgent indeed. It cannot be realistically believed that a society which is geared more and more to intellectual and technical competence will consider that so central a reality as healthy affectivity will be acquired automatically or at random by our youth. We cannot afford to conclude that love depends merely on the acquisition of a few principles that anyone with reasonable good will or intelligence will automatically absorb.

Love is, in fact, deeply influenced by the society in which it will be exercised. It is also called to purify that society, and to release it into its own greatness. An intelligent society moreover demands an intelligent love of its members, a love that

---

* Wilhelm Stekel, *Frigidity in Woman* (New York: Liveright, 1952), p. 19.

can reasonably exercise all the complex demands made on the person in structures of influence and uses of power. A twentieth-century society simply cannot be served by a vision of love that sufficed in the nineteenth. The terms of the engagement have changed; so have the range of powers available to man; so has the range of needs that call out to him.

Neither romantic love nor courtly love nor a love that is thoughtlessly bound to blood ties will be effective or indeed authentic today. The love which our century seeks is, in fact, a call upon one's whole being, a love capable of embracing the whole world. That world, as someone has observed, belongs, in fact, to the one who loves it most. Such a love engages one's entire personal resources. And though its activity is specified by the will, as traditional psychology teaches, yet the will must submit to a complicated play of reflection and judgment, of discipline and experience, of emotional freedom and restraint, in order to measure up to the demands of modern life, to offer something useful to it.

In the light of this, current emotional attitudes are in need of thoughtful re-evaluation. Often, in fact, our education seems to ignore the existence of emotional life, or compartmentalizes the emotions from mind and will, or implies that they need not be understood, and progressively freed and checked. Finally, there is a widespread incomprehension of the truth that the emotions stand at the heart of two essential aspects of human love: personality growth and the harmonizing of the physical and spiritual aspects of love.

It is also useful, in this regard, to reflect with Fromm that the prime concern of modern man is to be loved, rather than to learn how to love. To a notable degree, acceptance is the form that love takes, and to win acceptance, individuals attempt complete conformity—including scrupulous imitation of dress, manner and conversation, hobbies, common interests, and the acceptance of uncritical, middle-class rules of thumb.

"Relating" to others is studied with a seriousness that is sometimes comic, while the individual sources of warmth and strength are proportionately ignored. Popularity and sex appeal are considered intensely important and feverishly sought after, though the qualities that comprise them are stereotypes, profoundly rigid and dictatorial. Under these circumstances, the illusions of love tend to enlarge and deepen, under the fixation that love is a problem of the object, and not a problem of the subject. For the ordinary person therefore, love largely becomes a question of putting on the guises of love worn by others, because his theoretical and experiential equipment is unequal to the creation of his own form of love.

Fr. Ignace Lepp maintains that the problem of married love at its present crucial state is "one of integrating eroticism into marriage or marriage into eroticism." He believes that "the institution of matrimony has no chance for survival unless a successful integration of the two is brought about."* The new problem which life has brought to modern marrage can be seen in light of the contrast between man's technological sophistication on the one hand, and, on the other, his arrested or stunted emotional life. Men who marry are conscious of the great scientific and social achievements of our day, conscious, moreover, of having been a part of this development. Their wives, too, come to marriage determined not to surrender their personal autonomy. Such attitudes could be productive of immense marital good because they bring into marriage a dimension of self-reliance and human productivity largely lacking in the past. Yet the fact remains that the heightened consciousness and rich experience of contemporary men and women detracts from rather than contributes to eroticism as a human act, simply because they are not complemented by a proportionately maturing experience of

* Ignace Lepp, *The Psychology of Loving* (Baltimore: Helicon, 1963), p. 156.

community. Eroticism in marriage is meant by God to be both a cause and effect of communion, provided the partners bring to it the emotional and spiritual equipment which is infinitely more significant than mere sexual capability.

A few basic questions arise at this point. What sort of discipline is required of each partner to keep physical attraction alive? How does one develop the subtleties of understanding that preserve a spontaneous and welcome communication? What elements of maturity enable one to continue accepting the partner's limitations and failures while still conserving regard, love, and inner freedom? Indeed, it would seem that the issue here is not so much the education of married people, nor extensive help for the engaged. When people are about to marry, it is frequently too late for them to learn the responsibility needed for the married state. What would be immeasurably more useful would be a formation from early childhood stressing the discipline and rewards of love. In such a way, society would confront the alienation which is at present endemic among our young people.

III

The revolutions that are convulsing our society do not exempt the family from the assault against what has been tried or true or simply taken for granted. It must be admitted that the family is weathering the storm poorly, and is even losing ground, as forms of larger societies change and inflict their instabilities on the smaller groupings within them. Family instability must even in a sense be considered inevitable, given the revolution in human rights which has affected the traditional family structure, with its emphasis on human freedom. New views of the individual, new calls for equality and self-expression have seriously challenged the organic need of the family for order, restraint, law. The new tendencies ignore or lose sight of (one hopes only for a time) the older values of responsible individualism, duty, contribution to the common good.

One can recognize the gains that are implicit in many aspects of these changes, without in any sense being able to imagine what could substitute for the family itself. Even if no other voice were available to speak on behalf of the family, history itself would be a powerful witness to its value. Long before opportunities for schooling were at hand, the family nurtured its own special wisdom, and transmitted it; before there were special forms of social control, the family instilled a sense of order, and was, in fact, the chief pattern of social responsibility. And when modern societies began their painful journeys toward maturity, the family offered the necessary elements of support and preparation. Above all, in periods of history marked by wars, exploitation, plagues, and all the upheavals of social and political life, the family stood for continuity, peace, and human fulfillment.

Moreover, God Himself has sanctioned the human family, has entered it through the Incarnation, and has blessed it as a human form of life. "God is 'Our Father' and loves us 'as a mother the child of her womb.' Christ loves the Church, the 'mother' of His 'children,' as a man 'loves the wife of his flesh.' Since God elected to be born into a human family with all its relationships, the proudest of human titles ever bestowed is that of Mary, the Mother of God. And by the love of the 'Father and His only begotten Son' the concept of the family enters even the mystery of the Most Holy Trinity."*

The Christian dignity of the family is clear. At present, however, it is not precisely the status of parents or children that is challenged by ideological and social forces. It is the relationships that bind the family in unity. Parents, in the very immediate past, were everywhere regarded with respect as

---

* Marion Mitchell Stancioff, from a review of *Strangers in the House* by Andrew Greeley in *The Catholic Reporter*, Kansas City.

parents, though they might have been resisted as individuals. Now, to an ever-growing extent, the position of the parent is under fire; if some parents receive respect, it is because they have earned it, rather than because their status automatically warrants it. Obviously, there is both gain and loss here. To speak of gains, it is clear that parents could once play the tyrant without threat of challenge. Many homes, even in our recent past, were museums where the ego of a parent was the only exhibit, where the emotional growth of the children was crippled or stifled—even in the name of authority or religion or social status. It is interesting to observe how the three forces join hands in a novel like Dickens's *Dombey and Son*, perhaps the classic picture of the nineteenth-century strong man, whose family and workers both experienced the benign olympian, at work and at play. The children, of course, were not hoodwinked, as Dickens knew and as Dombey could never know. One of them, the Dombey son, found a way out simply by giving up the ghost in a domestic romantic opera. Other courses were open; the Dombey daughter, a tearful, unwanted sprite, went on to forbidden friendships with the servants. Dickens, who was an honest man, could see no other way open to the children of such a household. It was a domestic form of slavery that left few alternatives, even for his inventive mind.

Today, the old order is swept away, for good and bad. The new freedom, with all its changes for human development, with all its studies of child life and development, leaves many agonizing aspects of life without answer, leaves most parents in anguish before the world forces of development and disintegration. Children, too, from the time they begin to form attachments and to think for themselves, are cast on an open sea. In their search for guidelines, the young see values in the adult world which are more often opiates than sources of engagement. They see parental parochialism of all types, bounded for the most part by job and a circle of similarly narrow people. They see prejudice of all variety, and a determined defense against anything strange, different, or unwanted. They suffer the long silences between parents, the neurotically senseless quarrels, the infidelity to both family and marriage, and the sham of preserving a show of normalcy. Children see adults recoil from pain, demand, and effort; they are captive audiences to the crises caused by the disruption of routine, or by mood and vagary. With little of worth to find at home, the young go out in search of it. But having only a youthful version of parental values, they speed or drink or lose themselves in the meaningless release of vapid and unintelligible music. If these do not suffice, there is always sex. So the young, at the mercy of adults, are victims of shadowy ideals, of unstimulated and frustrated potentials, of dull and enervating boredom. And, above all, they are the victims of the impossible task of self-realization in a world which commonly neglects to recognize them, which refuses to lead them, and which is dreadfully afraid to use them.

One of the adverse effects of certain child-psychology texts has been the increase of parental "patience" with children. As the message goes, more time must be spent with children, and more care invested in their upbringing. Very little is said, however, of the quality of time or care, or of the child's ability to order himself and to develop his own sense of peace, with a minimum of intelligent direction. Consequently, parents are sometimes little more than victims of the whims and whines of their children; they are too ready with service, too lenient toward child monopoly of the home stage, which not only detracts from adult conversation, but often prevents the child from hearing anything worthwhile. Generally, children are encouraged by their parents to say too much, at the expense of education in the equally important business of listening.

Another example of indulgent treatment by parents is the obsessive exposure of children to what has been called "thing-addiction." From infancy on, many young people are confronted with the materialism of their parents. Food is rich, too ample, and is consistently wasted. Clothing is multiplied without need, toys proliferate within the home, often as means to keep the child quiet. The slightest material deprivation is viewed by parents with horror, as though no spiritual return could come from planned economy and encouragement to inventiveness. Later, allowances are granted, and many children work outside the home for money, doing the same chores that ought to be done at home for nothing simply because they too are responsible for their home. Parents, moreover, often underestimate their own young people; they do not offer a formation in responsibility toward others which is the great stabilizer of young lives. One thinks, for example, of the general lack of exposure to people of different races, and culture or lower levels of economic security. What a great contribution to family culture could be offered by the presence of thousands of foreign students in our country, or the millions of poor to receive and to befriend. Lacking such influences and constantly subject to ambiguous human relations at home, children grow up with a deep imbalance of spirit; they have been taught too long to rely upon things, and though unsatisfied with them they know nothing better than further pursuit of the familiar. After all, they think, money or a car or the latest style or this "steady" gives one evidence of belonging or prominence or mastery; and if they are the only experiences to which one can relate, why not try to build a world of them?

The full force of these family difficulties strikes at the adolescent. He often finds himself a stranger in his own house, caught in a distressing impasse. He is neither able to accept the adult values he sees, nor do without them. Though he rejects a home climate which he judges to be false, he cannot help but ape it, and repeat his teen-age version of the inconsistencies and denials of his elders. If dishonesty is common at home, why should he not cheat in school? If drink is a parental problem, the provocation of family dissension and violence, why not take the same escape? If sex at home is a subject for banter or the object of furtive planning and absence, why not try the same experiment? The burden under which the young labor today is a climate of immorality, not restricted to the home, a climate which often corrupts their ideals, saps their energies, and leaves them the prey of the very things they instinctively flee. In a land of plenty and beauty, in a civilization that has traditionally nurtured great men, young people today see scant evidence of heroism, much evidence of religious conformity, few people who are capable of understanding and love. More than one observer has appraised the situation and found it wanting: "Our boys and girls are handsome and strong, but they are wasting away within."

IV

The restless, evolving conditions of life make great demands on the quality of men and women. Human love finds itself challenged from two new directions. It must, on the one hand, grow in a sense of the person which will both protect and allow for development; on the other hand love is called to free itself from mere slavery to flesh and blood, to spiritualize itself by taking its stand with the whole of humanity. There is nothing new in all this, this has always been accepted in theory; all world religions and all classical theories on the nature of man have stressed both polarities of love, the personal and the universal.

But from another point of view, modern life has given both aspects a new possibility in hope and a new hardship in fact. Man has never, from a scientific point of view, known quite so much about the person—his psychological make-up, his power over the material world, his capacities for creation. And from another point of view man has never in history been so grievously threatened by forms of life and thought. Who, for instance, has lived for any time in one of our large cities without sensing to the heart the assaults upon his dignity, the attempts to erase whatever is unique in his being? And the world scene is hardly more reassuring. Wars have not only decimated whole populations and educated the young people of the nations to the blind folly of the science of sudden death, they have also created, at the heart of personal conscience, moral dilemmas that still, in this year, stand largely unresolved. Silence before crimes of genocide, thoughtless military service, questions of national loyalty, assail thinking men on all sides. And the traditional bulwarks of conscience—the churches, the systems of philosophy—have offered little help to conscience. Those who resist the drift of events do so largely on their own; and the masses and their institutions conform. So much, briefly and crudely, for the hardships, the obstacles that challenge a traditional view of life and love.

The opportunities are built into the very difficulties, as so often happens. For the first time in history, we have a hint before us of the vast possibilities that are open to men of love. We had always taught and thought that the world was made to the measure of man; that he was able to master it, make it his own. But the idea, if it is to mean something, is going to cost more than ever before in history. It is going to cost us many presuppositions, many built-in answers, many cozy attitudes. It has already cost uncounted lives; it is the kind of knowledge that has come to men in the fiery actuality of world hatreds and wars, and is coming home to them in an entirely new way in the possibility of world extermination of man. Love or perish; it is not a new commandment but its full impact was hidden from us, because we had not known, up to the recent past, that we were capable of mass murder and even of cosmic murder. We did not know what lay at the other end of the horizon where our love had not penetrated, because the full knowledge of man's destructive and creative power—both joined in his scientific breakthrough—was hidden from us. Now the veil is lifting from creation; we know that God has placed infinitely more of creation in our hands than we had dreamed; that our fate is literally in our own hands; that His Providence does not consist in a distant benevolence, but in our own willingness to grant Him entrance to the world, or to deny Him entrance, in the form of conscience.

In this sense, the problems we face, in their crushing, brutal, military form, or in their racial form, cast an entirely new light on the Gospel. They place the words of Christ in the breach in an entirely new way. And their pressure is so great on the traditional forms of His message, on the "Word of God" and the "deposit of faith" that we risk entirely mutilating His will unless we bring to bear on revelation the conditions of the actual world, the obstacles and opportunities which the world offers our ideal of love.

The question of atmosphere, of the mysterious power of example, of the style of life is extremely important to the family. It is something that can much more easily be sensed than defined. It would include, certainly, the capability of bearing with the day-to-day routine and the abrasions which life shared inevitably brings in its wake. More positively though, one must include the ability to shed a sympathetic light on the difficulties of the partner, to meet the needs of the other for mental growth and emotional maturity, to keep the marriage growing both outward and inward. All this requires a courage of a very high order. Most marriages, in fact, succumb, not to sudden or spectacular crisis, but to the numbing death of impersonal routine. The partners fail to understand what is required of them, once the first romance is over; they fail to understand that the marriage cannot continue to live indefinitely from its accumulated interest, but that it must invest again and again in the capital of altar and community, must summon the energy which only sacramental and world dedication can offer.

Such a sense of personal values is obviously lodged somewhere in the vision of life which each partner brings to the marriage. Only mature persons can face a modern marriage, which is quite literally a casting off into the deep; and this, not in a vitiated romantic sense of casting off the moorings of discipline and mutual respect and the spirit of sacrifice. What is in question is a view of human love which, long before the marriage experience, has already tested itself in mature life; in love, in community effort, in the discipline of serious tasks.

In the sense we speak of, the best preparation for marriage is the taste of life itself, not merely at the lips, but in the heart and mind. Perhaps a less valuable emphasis has been to concentrate too strongly on a specification of love, rather than a universal training in it and application of it. We stress, therefore, through ethics and negative norms, a specific love for marriage, one for friendship, one for this or that type of human need. In support of this approach are several underlying assumptions which bear investigation—namely, that it is soon enough to love when the "problem" dictating love is already present; and that, in some way or other, people can be fully human even before they are called upon to love. Under scrutiny, both premises prove highly questionable. One must assert, on the contrary, that a fundamental education in love is simply a human need, is essential to both man's reflection and experience, is simply part of his human make-up.

We are here speaking of a fraternal love which moves man to respect and serve, both as a supreme human value and as a personified way to God Himself. Fromm would explain this fraternal love as "the sense of responsibility, care, respect, and knowledge of any other human being, the wish to further his life."* Exclusiveness cannot be a part of such a view; rather its emphasis is upon common origin, common nature, common redemption, common rights, common destiny. Differences among men who admit such a view tend to diminish before the overwhelming evidence of human unity. Even such profound factors as religion, color, or degrees of intelligence appear secondary to the conviction that what may seem to separate men, class from class, race from race, is in reality an enrichment and deepening of their unity. And so the fraternal relationship moves not from periphery to periphery, but from core to core. Simone Weil expresses this with beauty and conviction: "The same words (e.g., 'I am your friend') can be commonplace or extraordinary according to the manner in which they are spoken. And this manner depends on the depth of the region in a man's being from which they proceed without the will being able to do anything. And by a marvelous agreement they reach the same region in him who hears them. Thus the hearer can discern, if he has any power of discernment, what is the value of the words."†

In a Christian view of things, the love of friendship is illumined and deepened by the example of Christ, and it is from Him that we have a basis for love's particular fruits—married love, community responsibility, social justice, political realism. Furthermore, our faith does not allow us merely to accept Christ in theory or as a general norm of conduct. He is, in fact, something entirely other—at once universal, liberating, and personal. How else but through Him can we seize upon the opportunities life offers, often in a bewildering, sudden,

* Erich Fromm, *op. cit.*, p. 39.
† Simone Weil, *Gravity and Grace* (New York: G. P. Putman's Sons, 1952), p. 117.

unrehearsed way? How else, except through His mysterious energy, can we expose ourselves to the agony of self-knowledge, to the unremitting war against egoism, to the acceptance of suffering, to the demands of service, to fortitude in failure? Truth must be earned, it is said, but love must be learned. And since love in the most realistic and ultimate sense is a Person, and begins and terminates only in the person, the whole course of the Christian is clear. Love proceeds through Christ and in Him.

Christ, therefore, must be learned as the most profound definition of every human being, a single image among many images, the soul within our soul. In Him all fullness dwells, as St. Paul says, in Him all things hold together, reconciled through the Blood of His Cross. Without Christ, we are like matter without form, persons without identity, the "hollow men" of T. S. Eliot.* With Him, we discover both ourselves and our world, penetrating His Death, Resurrection, and Ascension—living the Cross, sharing in His Life, more fully taking captivity "captive" by the fragmentary and momentary triumphs over evil in and around us, triumphs which will explode into the glory of the King of Heaven and earth. The integrity of our personality has its source in Christ, Who contains man as the "firstborn" of every creature, who heals man in Himself, who consummates him in the Divinity. Man indeed begins the task of becoming fully human when he undertakes the full acceptance of Christ, not merely as one among others to be admired or imitated, not merely as a great figure of history, but as God drawing his human life into the mystery of God. It is a simple, literal truth, finally, to say that only He can help us to accept our brother or restore our families, because only He can heal our inner lives.

Union with Christ is begun, continued, consummated in the

* T. S. Eliot, from the poem "The Hollow Men," *The Complete Poems and Plays* (New York: Harcourt, Brace and Co., 1952), p. 56.

Church, which extends in time the existence of the Saviour. And within the Church, the Liturgy portrays His great acts; it is a kind of contemporary epiphany of the Son of God to the world. But more than a manifestation of the Lord, the Liturgy is His saving action, the living out of His service of the Father in the members of His Body, the Redemption at work, with all its connotations of adoration, service, and penetration of society. Here are all the phases of the return to God of our world and of all time, here "the eager longing of creation" is loud, the Incarnation, the clash with Satan, the Death, Resurrection, Ascension and Advent of the Spirit are made present in mystery. Here Love is personified, the issues explained, perspective given, values established, power communicated. "You have not chosen me, but I have chosen you" (John 15:16). "And to one he gave five talents, to another two, and to another one" (St. Matthew 25:15). "I am the vine, you are the branches" (John 15:5). "If anyone love me, he will keep my word" (John 14:23). "Go you also into the vineyard" (St. Matthew 20:4). "Father . . . that they also may be one in us" (John 17:21). "All power in heaven and on earth has been given to me. Go, therefore . . ." (St. Matthew 28:18). In the Liturgy, the seeker hears once more the invitation of Christ to Andrew and John, "Come and see" (John 1:39).

And at the heart of all Liturgy is the offering of Christ, renewed at Mass. "But I have a baptism to be baptised with; and how distressed I am until it is accomplished" (Luke 12:50). And in our turn, sacrifice is an education in validity; it defines us as we are, it is the truest gesture possible to us. Moreover, it is the test of our will to become true followers of Christ. In response to the Eucharist, the soul of man focuses itself upon God in an attitude of dependence, the body follows soul in its own response to truth, the person stands before God as a being in search of unity and peace. What fol-

lows this simple presence of love to love offers an endless
variety of affective richness—consciousness of human worth,
openness to grace, purity of love, reawakened values,
strengthened hope, reform and transformation. We stand
before God in truth, stripped of all falsities, of the graven
images that we erect within ourselves, of the romantic masks
that we have assumed. Our dependence, our sonship, is the
form of our love, a love that would include and penetrate our
every faculty and raises on high our every resource and gift.

To specify the Ordinary of the Mass, to extend and enrich
its splendid tones of contrition and adoration, are the prayers
of the Proper. The Ordinary announces the Passion, Resurrection, and Ascension of Christ in terms of sacrifice, new life
and triumph; in it, the cycle of Christ's destiny enfolds us. But
the Proper extends this timeless redemptive action in all its
rich particulars; it brings home to us the Words and Actions
of Our Lord. The Mass may be of a saint or season; still the
Church speaks forcefully of "Jesus Christ is the same, yester-
day and today, yes, and forever" (Hebrews 13:8). Here is
the integrating force of the Saviour at work, the only Life
worth living. Here are His principles extended, realities illumined, the mystery of life and death relieved of its bitter
darkness. The Word made Flesh is present for our imitation;
but much more, His life joins our own.

In the Liturgy, Christ lives His Life once more, in us. And
we are the Church. What is asked of us at the altar, is that we
submit our lives to His by the precious paradox of finding
ourselves through an accepted loss. "He who loses his life for
my sake . . . will save it" (St. Mark 8:35). "Unless a grain of
wheat falls into the ground and dies, it remains alone" (John
12:24-25). If human relations be difficult, if frustration, sin,
and suffering are everywhere, if self-knowledge remains elusive, the main lines of solution, the courage to live with problems are here, in His Life. So is the connection between wor-

ship and life in the example He offers us. Indeed, the man whom the Liturgy has formed does not consider human life a thing apart, nor the Liturgy a principle of merely individual life in God, but rather a greater life finding expression in his own, as a stimulus for giving himself to others.

The Liturgy is both principle and power; in the Church, the Word of God is also a Presence, it is Truth embodied in One who exerts a dynamism which is divine. Our Lord makes available to us His own resources in the Sacraments, in the sacred signs which not only sweep us into His Being, but makes us partners to the same tasks of redemption. Without Him man can do nothing, with Him "greater [things] than these he shall do" (John 14:12). If the abuse of creatures has torn us from God and ourselves, then creatures—water, oil, bread—will be effective guarantees of reconciliation; what were instruments of chaos now become signs of peace. Bernard Haering, CSSR, has said that the "Christian community is the essential fruit of the Sacraments," and it is also true that the renewal of body and soul within the person is the result of sacramental action. Soul and body form a hierarchy and an integrity because Christ invades the personal structure and makes its work His own. He has killed our enmities in Himself, as St. Paul says, our enmities with God and with one another, but also within ourselves. "Peace I leave with you, my peace I give to you" (John 14:27).

A distorted image of reality is tragic enough in a single person, but particularly so in one who has chosen the vocation of marriage, since the loss of a sense of essentials in one partner can compromise and ruin the other. Married people have the power not only to make each other's life a passable version of Hell, they can literally damn each other. So the view of God and the world offered by the Liturgy seems crucial for them; it is accurate, integral, complete in depth and direction, gently healing. Moreover, the need of married people for a profound sacramental understanding and sharing is the more imperative, since the parish structure so often fails their deepest need for encouragement and growth. In this the Church shares with the civic community the questionable supposition that the married are adult and, therefore, self-sufficient.

This failure is sobering indeed in light of the grasp of marriage that the Church possesses and the tremendous riches that she can offer it. Our Lord has said that the truth will free us, and He sanctions that statement with all the wealth of His own love. The Liturgy offers both, and in the investigation of its social directions and implications, the family deserves prime consideration.

4. Racial Patterns and the Christian

In 1857, an abolitionist Negro named Frederick Douglass wrote the following: "If there is no struggle, there is no progress. Those who profess to favor freedom, and yet deprecate agitation, are men who want crops without plowing up the ground. They want the ocean without the awful roar of its many waters." America soon felt the prophetic force of these words, as the country erupted in the fratricide of Civil War. And now, a century later, the wheel of revolution has come full turn again; Douglass is as cogently relevant to 1965 as he was to the Civil War era, and America is discovering, in the most embarrassing fashion, that the War Between the States solved nothing—it merely began something.

The modern climate of revolution, of which the Negro revolution is but one among many, began with ideas—ideas of equality, ideas of material progress, of science and saving, of religious, political, and social thought. In our own day, men feel profoundly the necessity for such ideas, and the movements that may spring from them, as relief from conditions of life often intolerable, as means to self-realization and identity. By the same token, part of the process of emergence would be the necessity to challenge the obstacles to decency and a better life, those traditional and entrenched establishments of thought and system which justified preference and condoned exclusion of the great majority of mankind. The revolution of ideas, given life by World War II, has now bloomed into a struggle of "have's" against "have-not's," East against West, White against Black, and Christian against non-Christian—

changing ways of living, ways of regarding things, changing things out of recognition, and changing them with incredible speed.

So when Douglass spoke of the struggle necessary to pay for freedom his remarks went wider than the deprived condition of his people, wider than social turmoil for mere social ends—they were significant of the whole human condition and meaning. They suggest the price of being a man, but also the means to be a man: the constant struggle for the possession and free use of one's rights. This struggle is the price of freedom, which is never secure unless it is never taken for granted, unless it is repeatedly re-won after having been won.

Giving these considerations a national application to race relations, segregation is seen as an ugly and brutal contradiction: abuse of natural rights by whites, lack of natural rights among Negroes. Paradoxically, while possessing their rights, the majority of whites in this country are ignorant of the source of these rights, subvert them by making their use a prerogative of skin color, and narrow the boundaries of their own freedom by restricting the freedom of others. Professor James Silver of the University of Mississippi has asserted that the white Southerner is no more free than the Negro whose freedom he denies. In the Deep South, particularly in Mississippi and Alabama, whites have only limited freedom of dissent against racial custom, only limited freedom of association with those who may dissent, whether they be white or Negro. To speak out against racial crime, to expose the terrible oppression of the economic and social "system," this would invite precisely what the Negro receives as common diet, persecution and possibly death. In the North, the white atmosphere of indifference or ambiguous liberality does little more to promote true human freedom. Here, responsibility for justice is commonly seen as the precinct of government, of the churches, of the Negro himself. The two aspects of the spectrum contribute to a national climate in which white rights are the cause not of inner freedom, which expresses itself in responsible action, but inner slavery, since rights are not re-won by making them what they must be, a common property.

Perhaps an illustration or two will give clarity to what I mean. Both instances are true, both represent divergencies in the range of white attitude; both betray an ignorance which is entrenched and injurious. A Mississippi sheriff was supervising the dragging of one of the muddy state rivers (it might have been the Pearl River, which was repeatedly dragged for the three lost civil-rights workers), hoping to recover the body of a Negro, presumably resting on the bottom. The corpse was found finally and brought to dock, the wrists bound with chains, the feet lashed with chains, the whole body from head to toe circled with chains. The sheriff watched the proceedings with the same composure that he would watch the return of a dead rabbit by a retriever, and once his men were gathered on the dock around the dead man, he made this quizzical comment: "Now boys," he said, "ain't that just like a nigger—to get hisself more chains than he needs?"

Let us prescind from the barbarity of the scene and from the brutal epitaph offered a murdered man, for our story is a parable of many implications. The Negro's chains came to him with birth, and first they were figurative, but no less real. In Mississippi, considerable care was taken that he did not exist as a person (and this is an immense feat for any man, to exist while other men have decided that you don't exist). The white world into which he was born was erected morally, legally, and traditionally to secure him as a servant of the Southern "Way of Life"; it formed him to educational impotence; it fixed his boundaries of movement; it conditioned him to hopelessness; it made him a human starveling. Aldous

Huxley's *Brave New World* describes in frightful detail the careful preparation of a demimoronic class, destined to be the dispossessed tools of the social order, whose whole circuit of existence was defined by food, sex, sense pleasure, and robot-like tasks. Something similar was attempted with the Negro in the South; the chains were added one by one as life went on; the innocent optimism of childhood quickly evolved into a drab world of hopelessness and defeat. There came a time, however, in this particular case, when one too many chains were added; the burden became insupportable, causing the predictable reaction by the whites. Now the chains became literal, for there is nothing to do with a Negro who will not conform except to educate him further—to frighten him, to beat him, or if his case warrants it, to kill him. This Negro was killed.

Who then, became free, the Negro or his murderers? Freedom was the basic issue between them, yet under the circumstances, freedom was possible for neither. Whatever the Negro's fate, he was released for something better; while his persecutors, having denied their freedom by killing to protect it, chose a worse fate, the unfreedom of guilt and barbarism.

Recently, I had a long conversation with a prominent Northern businessman. He had been profoundly disturbed by the tactics of a civil-rights group in picketing the largest and best local hotel. He belonged to a group of wealthy people who ran the hotel as a joint venture, and they were very careful to conform the image of the place to the city it served—secure, placid, comfortable, and apparently fair in business ethics. The civil-rights people were attacking the hotel's policy of discriminatory hiring, and they began demonstrating with little preparation and with rather astonishing support from the townspeople.

The picketing began simultaneously outside the hotel, in a first-floor cocktail lounge, and in the lobby. There, the demonstrators accosted guests and diners, shouted their freedom songs, made impromptu speeches from the bandstand, intimidated the bellhops, and thoroughly disturbed the flow of business and the composure of management and guests. One diner was invited to reflect that his meal was supporting the hotel's injustice; another was kept from cashing a check in the lobby for twenty minutes by a picket line. A group of businessmen, furiously angry, stalked out of the cocktail lounge rather than risk loss of temper and a nasty scene. Almost immediately, the hotel management capitulated—they could not bear to have such obvious injustice publicized. But deep resentment remained among the involved whites; the outcome punished their personal pride and showed them the vulnerability of hypocrisy. Moreover, the experience revealed their moral convictions for what they were: "in support of human rights, but at no cost to themselves."

The inevitable clichés came up, moralisms whose limited truth hid the greater dimensions of responsibility. "You cannot fight injustice by infringing on the rights of others!" "Why will the civil-rights groups alienate the very people who want to help them?" And in the rationalization and excuse some very important questions were left unanswered. Why would a hotel run by Christian businessmen pursue discriminatory hiring, and why would the protest of demonstration be necessary to change this? Why would mature Christians be so absent from groups like CORE that tactics would sometimes be badly planned, causing unnecessary friction? What was known by the resentful whites in this case of the balance of justice and the redress necessary to restore it? Can Americans expect, with any sort of sensible realism, to wipe away the effects of three centuries of racial tyranny by a little Negro hiring, a few scholarships for Negro youth, a Civil Rights Bill? We still do not understand that our American standard of living has been built, to a great extent, on the

Negro's back, and that we have justified this by something that we have always disavowed, a caste system not only white, but select white. Who will pay for our historic blot of racism, which eclipses Hitler's slaughter of the Jews in ingenuity, in long-term ruthlessness, in numbers of people affected? Who will compensate for the dead children of Birmingham, for the dead civil-rights workers, for the hundreds of lynched, raped, starved, and murdered people, who suffer or die in silence? For myself, I do not know, for I see so few white Americans understanding, so few responding, so few paying. The immemorial blood and sweat and anguish of oppressed Negro millions will not be wished away because we would like it to be. America will have a race problem until we risk the formidable and painful task of restoring our personal integrity by extending justice to the Negro.

Presently, however, it is undeniable that we are fundamentally ignorant of the real issues in the struggle, and that we have a well-schooled talent for clouding the issues in favor of our convenience. The white backlash proves this, so does the superficiality of white judgment concerning the bad "tactics" behind the school boycotts and the World's Fair Stall-Ins, so does the rallying behind Governor George Wallace in Wisconsin, Indiana, and Maryland. To a great extent, it is not a question of our wanting what the Negro wants because his claims are just, it is a question of whether his claims are what we want. Even when one sees a modicum of good will expressed (good will can be painless; it can even be sought as a form of enlightenment), it is so often registered paternalistically, so often applied as the benignity of the "Great White Father," who indulges the undeserving child. Worse yet, and this inevitably happens when the Negro protest becomes irritating or threatening, there goes on in white minds the juggling of preferences, of priorities, and of conveniences. Are concessions to the Negro more painful, or are the inconveniences caused by his militancy more painful? It is a matter of taking the lesser loss; principle rarely penetrates such rationalization. It is a matter of temporizing and making peevish outbursts of self-justification, as though something were really being given, as though the guilt lay wholly with those who were asking for what was theirs.

II

Someone recently made the interesting observation that white America refuses, or is unable perhaps, to deal with the racial crisis in human terms. William Faulkner has certainly maintained this in relation to the South. There seems to be a note of defeat brought to the debate whenever it begins; the very terminology, white-Negro or white-black, introduces a focus disproportionate to its importance. When whites speak of Negroes, their notice is consistently concerned with difference—difference in the term Negro, and secondly, what Negro means to them, the factors of visibility, the myths and connotations connected with black skin. Granted that the very problem causes the terminology; yet mental adjustments are rarely practiced. The white will rarely say to himself: "I resent the terms of this debate; I resent the conspiracy which forces me to discuss this human being as white America discusses him, as Negro first and person second." Most white people eventually get around to the subject of the Negro these days, but there is little awareness that the polarities used in conversation (white-Negro) carry the divisions of race further; and that discussion, normally entered for enlightenment or solution, seldom achieves anything but a solidifying of white bias.

Because whites insist on regarding him as "different," the Negro has no choice but to react in defense, seeing the white as different also, and speaking of him as the "White Man," or "The Man." The white believes, with profound conviction, that the Negro is America's problem or the community's problem or someone else's problem, but seldom his problem. And never will he believe that he is the Negro's problem. Whereas, the Negro knows that the white is his problem, and that he has no other. In fact, Negro hopelessness, when it is encountered, centers on the fact that he is fenced in and engulfed with white "problems," more than one hundred and fifty million of them, and his despair arises from the fact that there are just too many.

This habitual incapability of dealing with the race issue in human terms will illustrate itself in the recent analyses of Negro militancy from the white community. Whites will rail out against Negro "irresponsibility"—the sit-ins, stall-ins, work stoppages, school boycotts. The New York press will relate with horror the fact that Malcolm X has advised Negroes to join a rifle club; it will devote extensive coverage to the largely nonexistent Blood Brothers of Harlem; it will grossly overplay Communist influence in the civil-rights groups—all with a gravity that reminds one of credulous children. Editorials, since the passage of the Civil Rights Bill, will speak seriously of the time for Negroes to "stand up and be counted," to prove their right of citizenship now that the country has guaranteed that right by law. National groups— Irish, Italian, Polish, and German—fresh from their own struggle for acceptance, will maintain loudly the Negro's need for the same experience, in wholesale admission that they know little of what the Negro has been experiencing for 350 years. Everyone in the white community, it seems, is ready with opinion, with advice, with tailor-made solutions; as ready to disavow incomprehension and guilt as they are loath to assume responsibility.

Perhaps a little second thought might be inspired by a few reflections on the course of the civil-rights revolution in the last ten years. For Negroes, the Supreme Court decision was a kind of Declaration of Independence; it was a new milestone in the process of equality that began with Lincoln's Emancipation Proclamation in 1863. It may be that no court ruling in our history was more significant for the country at large; but to Negroes, it gave rise to an enormous surge of expectation—something was going to happen to better their lot, and it was going to happen quickly. Expectation revived, and became both the greatest spur and the greatest frustration to Negroes.

There began, with the highly principled decision of the Court, certain signs that the days of Jim Crowism were numbered. The Federal and State Supreme Courts contributed by tumbling the old laws as fast as they were challenged; scientists were speaking out and saying that the Negro was equal and, that in human terms, the concept of race was meaningless; Negro athletes were becoming more prominent in the sports world; new responsibility was operating in the nation's businesses, and here and there, Negroes were stepping behind the desk and into the laboratory; a few Negroes were moving into white neighborhoods in the North, and seeing no housing panic follow their action; interracial marriages were still very rare, but evident enough to illustrate prerogatives of human choice; the emerging nations of Africa were making autonomy theirs at the stroke of a pen and the raising of a new flag; while finally, as the most powerful thrust to expectation, the communications media battered the Negro with proof that he was still a "have-not" whose citizenship and status had been put off to some unforeseeable future when it was convenient to give it to him.

Under these conditions, and the Civil Rights Bill is doing its work in this regard, expectation did far more than double or triple, it multiplied over and over again, and still relentlessly snowballs. Waiting in these circumstances ("wait" is the most common message that the Negro receives from the white community) becomes something of a school of desperation, the main prospect of a life that faces little but no-exit signs, little but the fences that make a world of deprivation and ghetto. Dr. Martin Luther King, Jr. speaks of the conflict between waiting and expectation in his *Letter From a Birmingham Jail*:[*]

> We have waited for more than 340 years for our Constitutional and God-given rights . . . I guess it is easy for those who have never felt the stinging dart of segregation to say "wait." But when your first name becomes "nigger" and your middle name becomes "boy" (however old you are) and your last name becomes "John," and when your wife and mother are never given their respected title "Mrs." —and when you are harried by day and haunted by night by the fact that you are a Negro, living constantly at tiptoe stance . . . and plagued by inner fears and outer resentments; when you are forever fighting a degenerating sense of "nobodiness"—then you will understand why we find it difficult to wait.

Moreover, the record tells us that the isolated progress of ten years did little more than prompt expectation, it did not change the general condition of the Negro. The fact of the matter is, there are now more Negroes in segregated schools than in 1954, there are greater numbers of Negroes unemployed than in 1954, there is more segregated housing in this country than in 1954. In short, the position of the Negro in American life has not really improved since the Supreme Court decision; it has gotten worse. With a view to Negro progress, the main fruit of this decade has been a growing gap between what the law says the Negro should have and what he has. This has been the only notable change.

[*] Dr. Martin Luther King, Jr., *Letter from a Birmingham Jail*, in *Black, White and Gray*. (New York: Sheed & Ward, 1964), pp. 67-68.

The Negro knows this, and knows it well. And when he looks back upon ten years of non-violent action, ten years of jail, countless physical outrages and beatings, firehoses, dogs, bombings, night raids, murders, millions of dollars spent in fines and bail—all this has resulted in no major breakthrough in any Southern city; while in the North the measures to push Negroes to the wall are more subtle and intense, what is the Negro reaction to be? What would the white reaction be, what would the human reaction be, given the same cruel history, the same heroic tolerance, the same consistent decision to challenge racism non-violently? Certainly, one could logically and fairly expect a growing disenchantment among Negroes, taking the form of talk about the feasibility of limited forms of violence, civil dislocation, etc. Certainly, there would be an agonizing questioning both of the theory of non-violence and the non-violent leadership of the civil-rights groups. The Negro knows that King, Farmer, and Rustin are pacifists; that Randolph is a pacifist in practice, if not in theory; that Wilkins and Young are concerned with legal and economic justice primarily; while Lewis and Forman have been drawn into non-violence by the orientation of CORE (Congress of Racial Equality) and SCLC (Southern Christian Leadership Conference). It seems to me that we cannot realistically expect Negroes to be non-violent supermen within a status of inferiority, particularly when one is familiar with the shallow record of non-violence over a decade.

Where has non-violence taken us? This is the question with many of the Negro militants. The truth is that it has not taken the Negro far, as a Negro. It has taken this country far; Negroes have for ten years been the greatest indictment to the American conscience; Negroes have shown the most striking examples of suffering for a principle and have offered major evidence of heroism; Negroes have forced America into the debate of human rights; and Jews, Puerto Ricans,

recent national immigrants, even some poor whites and migrant workers have benefited immeasurably from this debate;
Negroes have led the churches from the lethargy of institutional religion to a concern with people and their social condition; Negroes have done more for ecumenism in this country
than any other force, since Christians have partly forgotten
denominational differences under the stress of confronting a
purely moral problem; Negroes have shaken the whole massive and complex governmental, economic, and social structure of this country, compelling it to look at itself, compelling
it to admit that as it stands now it has neither adequate room
nor provision for people other than whites, and that this reality cannot remain. But all this has not changed the Negro's
condition, and he knows that once he ceases to be "the" news
item, once he stops protest and agitation (even the gimmicks
of bad tactics), once he terminates his belaboring of government, unions, and churches with the spectacle of his mal-
treatment, then everything stops; the whole country goes
back to its somnolence, its pietism, its childish seeking of
childish diversions.

Yet these realities, though appreciated by the Negro, are not
his objectives. He is not foolish enough to pose as a prophet
exposing his country's shortcomings; he want his rights; he
wants the status of an American; he wants his rightful slice of
this America for which he has suffered so grievously and contributed to so magnanimously. His revolution is directed not
to overthrow the system, but against the system, that he may
enter it. And in this, he has been largely unsuccessful.

Where do we go from here? This is what Negroes over the
land, North or South, are asking. The present stalemate in the
Negro condition can be largely found in the regrouping of
Negroes who reject non-violence, and whites who unalter-
ably oppose his rights. A far left and a far right have developed with amazing speed, and the ordinary Negro is caught

between. On the one hand, there is Malcolm X, the Muslims, black nationalist groups like ACT and RAM (Revolutionary Action Movement), talking about anything from the black state to the violence which whites find so frightening. On the other hand, there is the Ku-Klux Klan, which now operates both North and South under a cloak of respectability, the Citizens' Councils, the Rev. Billy James Hargis' Christian Crusade, the Americans to whom Governor Wallace makes sense, the far-right segment of Senator Barry Goldwater's support. The two extremes have noticeably reduced the maneuverability of the established civil-rights groups, have notably lessened their voice and the respect in which they were formerly held.

It is a fact fearful enough to give us serious pause, that our uncomprehending and stubborn face to the Negro is literally driving him to the irresponsibility of which he is so often accused. In fact, it would seem that Christian honesty would demand our analysis of this word irresponsibility, which we sometimes apply to the Negro in the most irresponsible fashion. Negroes have every right to ask, "Responsible to whom?" and also, "Who has been responsible to me?" We have never been Christian enough, or American enough, to tell the Negro that we believe in him, though we have been very ready to demand his belief in us. The Negro has placed at the disposal of this country one of the triumphal episodes of human responsibility—in slavery, in the Reconstruction Period, in the great wars of America, in the building of the nation, in the present revolution for human rights. None of us has a prior right to citizenship; few of us have invested in this soil as he, in suffering, sweat, and blood; all of us will realize ourselves in God and country only because he is here. The charge of Negro irresponsibility is a historical lie, the truth of our irresponsibility is an overwhelming fact.

III

It would be accurate to state, perhaps, that most Americans, white or Negro, are ignorant of the human damage that comes from the inhumanity of segregation. Both persecutors and the persecuted suffer, and racial conditions being what they are in this country few are exempt. It is, therefore, a most controversial point: Who is most degraded by Jim Crowism, white or Negro? In the case of the first, one sees developing an inflation of worth arising from a false sense of superiority, which involves the person in complicated areas of delusion, rendering normal human relationships terribly difficult. In the case of the Negro, the opposite polarity is established. For our purposes, however, a focus upon the Negro is more important, since whites have more access to the means of remedy, while Negroes do not, their rights being the only remedy.

Fundamental to this complicated and malignant disease that is called segregation is the myth of color and the consequent identification of status with a white skin. Concepts and values like these have so divided the races that whites are generally unaware of what it means to be a Negro and what the Negro must endure through the kind of half-life accorded him in this country. Moreover, segregation by its very nature robs the white of any desire to learn (as John Howard Griffin learned) about the abject wreckage that can consume Negro lives, because there is so often denied them the common sources of hope, readily available to most whites.

The American Negro is the product of a splintered culture, essentially Anglo-Saxon and white, but adulterated in his regard, by the reality of majority standards, minority means. The Negro had no say about his presence in America, no say about the values imposed upon him, no say about the quality or quantity of means to attain these values. Because of his skin and the status joined to that skin, he became and still is the

American foreigner, the citizen whose presence goes back to the historical roots of national life, yet whose person and lineaments have been so befouled and stigmatized that he is still unhome in this country.

His life, as Americans define it in its implications of misfortune and deprivement, was first defined by a myth as absurd and pernicious as any history records, the myth of race. We are indebted to a Frenchman, Comte de Gobineau, whose "Essay on the Inequalities of the Races" was published in this country in 1856, to support the cause of slavery. Later, it was used in Germany as a remote authority for Hitler's doctrine of Nordic superiority. At any rate, it is only recently that anthropologists have emerged from a cocoon of impersonal preoccupation to speak forcefully about race, and to say that "scientifically, there is no such classification as 'race' based on pigmentation." For all practical purposes, "race" is a myth that has caused enormous harm. Race relation is about four hundred years old and was developed to justify slave labor. "Every premise of the myth—its ostensible scientific jargon, its specious moral philosophy, its fabricated moral antecedents—are as false as the myth itself."

But to the Negro, the myth has been large as life itself—it followed him as closely as the skin with which it was one; there was no relief from it, and few reminders that it was not so. It became a construct into which he had to fit his life, and it bred a caste system which told what he was not; what he could not do when he had the right to do this; where he could not go when he had the right to go there. People everywhere, it is true, sometimes choose to live a lie, this being part of the human condition. But Negroes must live a lie, at least in appearance, and though they might miraculously achieve an inner integrity, this would be possible only because of a torturous denial of what society told them they were, plus detachment from the part society expected them to play.

Because of the figment of race, the Negro has had no general choice but to adjust to the image of white prejudice—it was either adjust or die. The reasons for this are rooted in slavery but the Negro position during Reconstruction sufficiently explains his present dilemma to restrict ourselves to this period.

When the Negro was "emancipated" following the Civil War, he was given a mobility of status that was in name only. This status was, above all, dependent upon force; it was grudgingly given by Southerners, and it was, therefore, in constant jeopardy. Moreover, the Negro was psychologically unprepared to receive it. Then, as now, two perennial questions needed answering to clarify Negro relationship to the remainder of Americans. First, could he rise to reciprocal relations with the white community; and secondly, was he ever given the opportunity to try? The answer to both questions was and is, no; because it was impossible to relate to the whites on the basis of equality. To put it technically, there was no "reciprocal emotional interaction" between the races. The imperative move in this context was the white overture toward the Negro, the emotional transition needed for full acceptance of the Negro. To a vast extent, whites have always refused to do this. Consequently, discrimination appears in any variety of forms. It is apparent that whites have made reluctant compromises in the face of multiple domestic and international pressures, including Negro militancy. But the history of the Negro in slavery, since the Civil War, and even today, speaks of accommodation to the conditions that the white man has chosen for him. The moral and political voice of the Negro grows apace, yet whites are showing themselves both ingenious and ruthless in keeping him a stereotype of convenience.

An over-all look at the current predicament of the Negro is our society will give some explanation for the traumatic effects of the calculated and generalized dehumanization that is segregation. The Negro earns today less than 53 per cent of the white per capita income; as 10 per cent of the national population, he has an unemployment ratio triple that of whites (12 to 4 per cent); conservatively, two-thirds of all American Negroes are impoverished. Moreover, his economic position is worsening. In 1947, the non-white unemployment rate was 64 percent higher than the rate for whites; in 1963 it was 124 percent higher. On the average, the non-white college graduate can expect to earn less than the white pre-high-school dropout; while he will earn only 47 percent of the white college graduate—in terms of a lifetime, $185,000 to $395,000.

The work of the Negro, for the most part, is concentrated in the lowest paid and most menial occupations, carrying with them long and strenuous muscular effort, the greatest physical danger, the greatest subjection to injury, and generally, less pay for the same work done by whites. He is often a day or a week worker, having no control over work policy or productive means; and he is least found in jobs that are rewarded with an annual wage, that is, the professional or managerial echelons. If he enters into business for himself, it is because he has saved his money (he often cannot borrow it), and he must generally go into areas where no competition with whites exists, the so-called personal service fields—barber and beauty shops, cleaning and pressing establishments, funeral parlors, and the like. And even in these, he finds little economic security, since 85 percent of Negro businesses are one-man and owner-operated, and many pay so poorly that a second job must be maintained. Finally, no one has suffered from automation as has the Negro, and if there was any doubt before, automation has literally shown him to be the "last hired and the first fired."

According to his white judge, the Negro is expected to hurdle another obstacle in educational deficiency, and if white reasoning were analyzed, it would go something like this: Negroes are expected to put up with inferior schools, which are deliberately kept inferior through segregation, yet they are expected to become educated in spite of what has not been taught. Then, in case some become educated (and some Negroes do, in spite of the common impregnability of the separate but unequal school system), they are firmly kept in place, because, after all, they are niggers. Or to put it differently, Negroes are smugly advised to lift themselves up by their educational bootstraps, but there is a great silence when it comes to provision for doing this, or recompense once the rare feat is accomplished.

There has been incessant litigation over the schools for ten years following the Supreme Court decision, but of nearly 3 million Negro students in the eleven hard-core Southern states, less than one-half of 1 percent now go to school with white students. In the North, school segregation is more and more the fact, as housing segregation takes an increasingly obstinate pattern. It is rank understatement to say that the almost universally segregated Negro system is inferior. The greater number of Negro Southern schools are not accredited, and their per capita budgets hover anywhere from 20 to 40 per cent of state allotments to white schools. The buildings are often decrepit, poor in space and teaching aids. The teachers have been produced by the same system as their pupils; they are subject to intimidation by the local oligarchy; they are apathetic and deficient in knowledge and experience. In country areas, many children do not finish elementary school; while in both Northern and Southern cities, with emergence into high school, the pressure upon students to quit becomes enormous. Lower-class Negro students cannot relevantly relate school to the future, because almost by rule, it is irrelevant. There is usually nothing to be ambitious about. Within the family, or in the neighborhood, ample evidence is at hand that the future is a dim prospect, while the present offers the street and with it, opportunity for adventure and sexual experience.

The constitution of the Negro family is another instance of the abrasive influence of segregation. Under slavery, the Negro woman was the dominant figure in the community, because of the common practice of white males who were quite color-blind when it came to illicit sex. (Concubinage between white women and Negro men was not as common, though not at all negligible.) Negro women, through the sexual relationship with the dominant whites, gained an emotional hold over their paramours, thereby piercing the caste system to a limited degree and gaining concessions for themselves and their children. Negro men, on the other hand, were far more expendable; they could be sold alone or shifted alone; they did not need to be considered to the same degree. This system of female priority perdured with the family in the postwar years; the dominance that Negro women had gained under slavery continued with her greater value as a provider. This dominance possessed, of course, its psychological counterpart—Negro women felt themselves superior to their men. Later on, when the migrations to the North began, it was common for Negro men to go first, leaving their wives behind to keep the family; but also to allow them to deepen further the worst elements of the matriarchal structure. There is reason enough for the difficulty that Negro women have had to retain respect for their men, who received far harsher treatment from the whites; who had far inferior economic opportunity and, therefore, less chance to qualify as breadwinners; who were far more prone in their discouragement to seek the common escapes, such as desertion, infidelity, alcohol, and so on. Life being what it is, Negro men have never generally been able to inherit their manhood; they could never sufficiently assert their masculinity so that it would give them stability and self-respect.

Consequently, the uterine family is the rule with the Negro poor, less and less as the earning power of the father increases. But within the matriarchy, the hardworking, fatigued, and irritable Negro mother is all too common, who demands instant obedience of her children, who is harsh in punishment and sparing of affection, who loves her children without having the energy to express it. The effects of such an atmosphere are humanly disastrous—early neuroticism of various types, jealousy and conflicts among the young, little common life, and strenuous efforts by the males especially to emancipate themselves at the first opportunity.

The caste system is another factor which helps to create within the Negro a sense of inferiority and dispossession. (Caste in its turn is instrumental in causing class among Negroes, which follows the lines of skin color, education, and earning power—in short, proximity to white standards.) Because of caste, however, Negroes are kept from intermarriage with whites; from common housing with whites; from cliques and clubs with whites; from fraternal orders and professional associations in the fields of education, social welfare, religion, medicine, art, and business—wherever exclusiveness is the object with whites, wherever white status must be protected and maintained. Negroes are allowed to participate in a relationship of sorts with white employers, but they are kept firmly in a subordinate position, and rarely is a Negro allowed to exercise authority over whites. It is little wonder that the all-pervasive and multi-dimensional "system," as it is called by Negroes, gives rise to despairing comments like the one a Southern Negro made to me several years ago: "Everywhere I go in this city, I am reminded that I am something less than a man and a full American. My neighborhood is segregated, and I know I could not buy out even if I had the money. I can't compete with white men of my education, because they're white and I'm colored. I don't have the political voice that I should have, though I vote regularly. I can't spend my money as I would like to, in fact, my dollar is worth less. I turn around and look and everywhere the fences are up. It's a hard life and it can only change for the better."

IV

Are we to assume that what the Negro has to endure in America develops a distinct personality? The question can appear ambiguous, but in comparison with those who are not under the burden of discrimination, the Negro does have a distinct personality. His situation in this regard rests upon the fact that the human personality has a tendency to form itself in reference to central problems, problems which force or invite adaptation. For Negroes there is only one problem—the others tend to dissolve themselves in this one—the problem of discrimination. All aspects of his life polarize themselves around the behavior of whites toward him. Nor can we honestly expect from him the capability to localize the psychological effects of discrimination, to reduce their influence, or to eliminate them. On the contrary, these effects are a constant and unrelieved irritant—they live with the Negro consciously and unconsciously, and are as much his companion as his name. To protect himself against these constant assaults upon his dignity, automatic and unconscious maneuverings are adopted, as much to preserve sanity as to allow life to go on with some sort of identity.

The great masses of the Negro race in this country live in such a total climate of repression that one is able to discern a consistency of reaction to white bias. (The same is true of middle- and upper-class Negroes, though reaction takes more subtle forms with them.) The total complex of discrimination forced upon the lower-class Negro imperceptibly robs him of self-esteem, which leads to contempt of himself and his race, with a contrasting and enormously exaggerated idealization of whites. This white ideal, foisted on the Negro through the everyday reality of segregation, is obviously an unattainable one; it is a dead-end street—no efforts to treat the hair or bleach the skin will suffice. They do not change the fact of being Negro. This impossible ideal, which he is not free to choose or reject, breeds hostility toward whites, but it is a hostility tempered by fear, since any expression of it will meet the harshest reprisal.

What is done with this ideal which can neither be gained nor repudiated? It is introjected, and comparisons are set up between what the white ideal is thought to be and what the Negro thinks himself to be. In his own estimation, the Negro suffers from this comparison, and what was first an inadequate self-esteem turns to self-hatred which, for mere purposes of release, is often cast upon other Negroes, who are seen as common partners in misery, and even causes of the misery. There is here at work a progressively dangerous and cumulative psychological poisoning, which is commonly the source of neuroticism like anxiety complexes, hypertension, and compulsive tendencies of various types. To a great degree, it is also behind psychosomatic illnesses like migraine headaches, high blood pressure, respiratory ailments, and skin diseases; a high incidence of escapism, manifesting itself through alcoholism (alcoholic psychosis is twice as common with Negroes as with whites), dope addiction, promiscuity and marital infidelity, family desertion, and general apathy; frequent anti-social behavior, exhibiting itself through unusual hostility toward other Negroes, a general suspicion toward white people, and an irresponsible disregard of the rights and property of others. Here we have evidence of human helplessness before what has been called "the conspiracy of dehumanization." We know it as segregation.

We are not to think, however, that the Negro is completely passive before the unvarying wall of white discrimination, any more than other humans would be so in the same circumstances. He is incessantly asking himself two questions as he attempts to adjust to and rise above his lot: What can I do to repair my injured self-esteem? What can I do to protect myself against further traumatic damage? What he does are the answers to these questions—flamboyant dressing, flashy cars, uninhibited dancing, straightening of hair, disparagement of others, "joining" of organizations, gambling, propensity toward religious quackery, excessive credit-buying. Or if something more positive is sought by way of answer, there is the response to humanity in others, vast tolerance and a deep sense of forgiveness, incredible capacity for suffering, instinctive sympathy with the more unfortunate, hope and humor and inexplicable optimism. All of these, it must be understood, are *human* responses to problems not of the Negro's making, and as such they are tangible evidences both of the human need for understanding and compassion, as well as the human triumph over injustice.

The psychological picture just dealt with changes to some extent with the middle and upper classes. The Negro poor, for the most part, are primarily involved with the fight for subsistence, while the upper classes struggle for status. With the latter, the same capacity for white idealization is present, though sharpened by better education, better family background, better and clearer goals. The ideal, however, continues to be white, continues to be beyond reach—the middle- and upper-class Negro can get a bit closer, that is all. However, the capability of effort and the proximity of the ideal makes the conflict more disastrous in its punishments. Expectation has become more vigorous as equality is approached, yet equality remains tantalizingly beyond grasp, an elusive and unattainable goal. The toll in frustration can be frightful, and often is. The white ideal, painfully near, yet perpetually beyond grasp, is hated and hatred causes guilt, which reduces self-respect and introduces resentment both against whites and against Negroes lower than himself. As one upper-class Negro said: "The only thing black that I like is myself."

So it is that middle- and upper-class Negroes hate whites as oppressors, but their hatred is well controlled and allowed to show itself only in a disguise of affability and good manners. This is a calculated process, since the preservation of status rests heavily on the preservation of good human relations, and one does not invite a disruption of relationship which, in turn, would cause a wider ostracism, added slights, and a general loss of hard-won ground. These dangers middle- and upper-class Negroes cannot risk, having already paid too much to avoid them. So appearances and conventionalities are maintained with the whites, while lower-class Negroes are disliked; and they are shunned as reminders of what might have been, as possible stereotypes which are best forgotten. Such attitudes toward other Negroes cause a deep sense of guilt impregnated with anxiety, since there is also at work a sense of loyalty to those for whom he feels responsibility. In the last analysis, the upper classes of Negro society have to exercise unremitting and painful control over emotional and psychic life, to the expense of spontaneity, self-confidence, and free relatedness to others, including other Negroes. So often, when it comes to a choice between spontaneity and further loss of self-respect, the Negro must discard the first, its loss being the lesser evil.

V

The guilt for all of this rests very heavily upon us, and the evidence of that guilt is displayed in every rightful Negro protest, in the need which makes demonstration necessary, in the violence of Harlem and Bedford-Styvesant, in the unsolved murders of the South, in the latent violence of black nationalism, in the ignorance and immobility of white America. "How is it that you do not judge this time?" (St. Luke 12:50). The signs of our time are what is happening in our streets; in the terror-ridden areas of the rural South; in the overcrowding, filth, and despair of Negro homes; in the arrogant and hypocritical preachments of well-fed, comfortable, and guilty white Americans. And the meaning behind the signs lies with those who persist in denying the Negro his God-given and legal rights; those who are heard from only when the Negro tries to open the door that has been slammed in his face.

"The conscience of the nation is on trial,"* the American bishops tell us. We are being asked today by God to wipe the slate clean, a history disfigured by 100 years of legal tyranny, brutalization, and denial of human dignity; and before that, more than 200 years of the horror of slavery. How many white Americans are willing to face a tribunal (either God's or man's) and accept complicity in this collective crime, which has despoiled the lives of millions of innocent people? We have been aghast at the genocide of the Nazis and the purges of the Russians, but there are pockets of wretchedness in Harlem and in the South that do not have the dignity of a gas oven. It has been remarked by Negroes, with the tart and bitter insight that comes from life, that "most pets in this country live better lives than most Negroes." We cannot say that we had nothing to do with this; we might not have been responsible for the causes of this immense human disaster, but we are responsible for its continuance. Again, we are welded together by Providence in this nation, and racism is our national cancer. More importantly, we are all members of the human family, and if we are to believe Christ and St. Paul's interpretation of Christ, the interests of all are the interests of

---

* Statement of the American Bishops, August, 1963.

every one, the rights of all are the rights of every one, the future of all depends on the present of every one. "Those who support racism by action or inaction betray Christ and the Fellowship that bears His Name."[*]

Therefore, it is infantile to say, "I have never known a Negro (or only a Negro maid or janitor)" or "Nothing but intermarriage will come of this" or "The Negro is going extremist or Commie." Statements like this betray the speaker, and expose his prejudice as stupidity, immaturity, and even malice. Above all, such statements show a placid refusal to learn why there is nothing against intermarriage, why the races are separated, why a few Communists have joined the Negro. The Negro has no esoteric ax to grind; he is not agitating (except in desperation) for a nationalism within the national framework; he is not even a lobbyist for special interests. He wants merely and simply to be treated as a human being, he wants to be received as a Christian and as an American, he wants what whites expect and get. W. E. B. DuBois spoke accurately for the aims of Negroes when he said: "We claim for ourselves every right that belongs to a freeborn American—political, civil, and social—and until we get those rights, we will never cease to protest and assail the ears of America with the story of its shameful deeds toward us."

I cannot honestly say that redress will presently be demanded of us by the Negro, who knows us too well to push his luck. Our society, moreover, has its own way of cushioning against any painful readjustment which might be necessary to right the wrongs of the past. However, any valid experience with the Negro, any Christian appraisal of what he has endured and still endures, any course of action that would insist upon justice now, any such approach would force us to view the Negro as the favored citizen that he is, and would lead us to put the might of our national intelligence and re-

* Statement of the National Council of Churches, August, 1963.

source at his disposal. But this is presently beyond us—our Christianity is not of the caliber to understand such realities. We can but concern ourselves with the possible, in the hope that the Negro be recognized as the American that he is, in the hope that the disgrace and horror of further bloodshed be avoided, in the hope that God will reduce the redress that He will most certainly ask. For the possible is always more than what is being done.

If I would venture any observation at the conclusion of this, it would be to draw attention to the central fault of which so many of us are guilty; the inability to project our lives into the lives of others, to inhabit the skin of another person, particularly the skin of those who do not possess the middle-class standards that so concern us. Partly through inadvertence, partly through refusal, we are very poor students of the human condition—our self-centeredness robs us of an objective gaze that is true and real. Consequently, we become victims of an impersonality that has little to do with the human scene as it is; experience with other human beings has not purified and balanced our grasp of reality. In these circumstances, the subjective becomes focal, a neuroticism of selfishness develops, and life becomes a history of catering to the peevish and inconsistent demands within us. Both Christianity and humanity are impossible under these conditions. This poisonous state becomes apparent in white reflections upon the Negro condition, reflections which are an almost total abstraction from an objective point of judgment, betraying in themselves an obdurant decision to justify oneself and to protect one's course in life.

The Negro says in point, "He thinks like a white man!" —and at work here are a variety of emotional and mental constellations, some of which bear mention. There is the imperceptivity on the part of the white of any condition of life save his own (or one quite like his own), which is the only one worth having, simply because it is his. There is the anxious resolve to protect this condition, which is idealized out of all proportion, and whose loss is viewed as unimaginable. (Hence the rote tendency to protect white "interests.") There is the irrational inclination to make exaggerated demands of the more unfortunate, demands far more stringent than he would ask of himself under the same circumstances. There is the superficial knowledge of what is meant by social justice, and particularly, what the Negro's inherent and legal rights are. Finally, there is the consistent denial of what charity is, with its emphasis upon personal worth, with its transcendence of legal rights and welfare programs, with its disregard of "irresponsibility" in its object, with its vital and centralized concern with this situation, this wrong, this person. Christ did not complain of improvidence before feeding the multitude; the Samaritan did not "investigate" before ministering to the injured Jew; St. Paul did not mention status or skin color when he said that we were members one of another. If the white man must learn anything, he must learn this: his only debt to the Negro is love; a love which is inescapable, too long unpaid, one which he owes to the Negro, but to himself as well. What comparison can be made between giving the Negro what is already his, and receiving, in turn, what he has to offer us? The Negro is offering us our humanity, because for white America Christianity is a burlesque without him. It is a fair trade, indeed, even in the face of the most calculating self-interest.

On the eve of the March on Washington, a great American died. He was a brilliant, sensitive, and turbulent individual, and the sufferings of his people in this country broke him to a degree, causing him to renounce his U.S. citizenship and embrace Communism for a time, and die in Ghana, a voluntary exile. He has been called the "Father of the Civil Rights Movement," and in spite of his alienation from this country and its Negro people, he did his work well. It was he, perhaps, who first saw the impossibility of the Negro's climb to full citizenship without his rights, and this point alone caused his break with Booker T. Washington and gave a new cast to the struggle. Dr. W. E. B. DuBois had a "credo" which I think is as stirring a piece as ever came from American literature, a credo which could purify our view of human rights, and thereby guarantee the future of the Negro:

> I believe in God Who made of one blood all races that dwell on earth. I believe that all men, black and brown and white, are brothers, varying, through time and opportunity, in form and gift and feature, but differing in no essential particular, and alike in the possibility of infinite development.
>
> Especially do I believe in the Negro race; in the beauty of its genius, the sweetness of its soul, and its strength in that meekness which shall inherit this turbulent earth.
>
> I believe in pride of race and lineage itself; in pride of self so deep as to scorn injustice to other selves; in pride of race so chivalrous as neither to offer bastardy to the weak nor beg wedlock of the strong, knowing that men may be brothers in Christ, even though they be not brothers-in-law.
>
> I believe in service—humble, reverent service, from the blackening of boots to the whitening of souls; for work is heaven and idleness hell, and wages are the "well done" of the Master who summoned all them that labor and are heavy laden, making no distinction between the black, sweating cotton-hands of Georgia and the first families of Virginia, since all distinction not based on deed is devilish and not divine.
>
> I believe in the devil and his angels, who wantonly work to narrow the opportunity of struggling human beings, especially if they be black; who spit in the faces of the fallen,

strike them that cannot strike again, believe the worst and work to prove it, hating the image which their Maker stamped on a brother's soul.

I believe in the Prince of Peace. I believe that war is murder. I believe that armies and navies are at bottom the tinsel and braggadocio of oppression and wrong; and I believe that the wicked conquest of weaker and darker nations by nations whiter and stronger but foreshadows the death of that strength.

I believe in liberty for all men; the space to stretch their arms and their souls; the right to breathe and the right to vote, the freedom to choose their friends, enjoy the sunshine . . . uncursed by color; thinking, dreaming, working as they will in a kingdom of God and love.

I believe in the training of little children, black even as white; the leading out of little souls into the green pastures and beside the still waters, not for self or peace, but for life, lit by some large vision of beauty and goodness and truth; lest we forget, and the sons of the fathers, like Esau, for mere meat barter their birthright in a mighty nation.

Finally, I believe in patience—patience with the weakness of the weak and the strength of the strong, the prejudice of the ignorant and the ignorance of the blind; patience with the tardy triumph of joy and the mad chastening of sorrow—patience with God.*

* W. E. B. Dubois, *Dark Water* (New York: Harcourt, Brace & Co., 1920), pp. 3-4.

5. Segregation and the
Nuclear Arms Race

Richard Carrington, in his *Guide to Earth History*, makes this interesting observation: "Let us imagine that by some magic the whole of the earth's history could be compressed into a single year. On this scale, the first eight months would be completely without life. The following two would be devoted to the most primitive of creatures. No mammals would appear until the second week of December. Man, as we know him, would walk on stage at approximately 11:45 P.M., on Dec. 31st. The age of written history would occupy little more than the last sixty seconds on the clock." A certain bogus humorist weighed this passage and made the following remark: "That ought to help you to reduce current world problems to the proper perspectives."

Current world problems, it is clear, are compounded in mankind; so it is of only the slightest import that man or his agonies can claim but an instant in the life process of our planet. Though we would sometimes prefer to treat humanity's anguish as an abstraction, or an offensive dream, it is clear that man's historical situation is real, present to him, and as present, capable of casting shadow or light on his future. Therefore, it is much more accurate to say that these "problems" are the universal and corporate symptom of man's illness or health. The symptoms are in the body and the body is our own. It is a Christian view, in fact, to maintain that human problems are a stimulus to growth, enterprise, and practical maturity; that without challenge, we have not life, but utter pointlessness and frivolity. In such a view, it would follow that the sufferings of the Harlem Negro or the starving Chinese peasant or the East Berliner are of far more import as symptoms of mankind than the querulous psychosomatic complaints of the affluent. Finally, it is pertinent to the Christian faith to insist that truly human problems are evidence of the unfinished human Redemption in its modern form, and that our Saviour is offering His maturity to man through the Communist, the Negro, the Cuban, through mankind in its efforts toward community.

In this light, Communism might be viewed as the reaction of an outraged humanity to our own deliberate secularism. The cold war is seen as a harsh, uncompromising challenge to our democracy, and beyond that, as a challenge to the validity of our Christianity. The arms race is an indictment of our pious, half-believed contention that moral strength is the strongest force in the world—a contention restricted to pharasaic preachments. Segregation is a symptom of our divided minds and hearts, which refuse the remedy offered to our inner division, in the acceptance of a Negro brother. Our declining family situation is the outgrowth of an illusory romanticism, inextricably tied up with the marketing of sex as part of the gross national product. In all of these national and worldwide problems there are patent evidence of our illness— "signs" like the ones the Jews sought from Christ. In this regard, Christopher Dawson speaks of a tyranny of thought in which national interest moves in the guise of personal benefit, in which the common good is abandoned as the province of law, in which the neighbor, wherever he may be, is considered only as an instrument of self-aggrandizement.

I would like to consider two questions which seem to me particularly indicative of our malady and illustrative of the direction that our action must take. I refer to national segregation and the international arms race. It may become clear in the course of reflection that these two are related problems and that segregation is psychologically creating a climate in which our massive reliance on nuclear weapons may flourish. It may become obvious that we as a people are losing more and more command of our own morality, and that it is being more and more dictated to us through our refusal to accept others. It may become obvious that the tyranny that we impose upon our own citizens, one-tenth of our population, has now threatened to take an international form in the larger neighborhood of the world. It may become obvious that human injustice is no longer content to take specialized forms, or to exist under local restrictions, but like a Hydra contrives a new face for every area of the world. It may become obvious that the commonly dispassionate decision of the American people to relegate the Negro to the cellars and slums of American life makes it not only easy but logical to enlarge our oppressions in the form of international nuclear threats. I submit that the two phenomena, segregation and the arms race, are very much connected and that the vicious seeds of one help to promote the other; and that, conversely, if we solve our national segregation problem, we will gain strength to pursue avenues of action on the international scene which will further our Christian integrity and insure the peace.

II

There is emerging from the debate and painful spectacle of the civil-rights struggle certain phenomena, one of which is the enormous difficulty of projecting and receiving the objective picture of Negro-white relationships in this country. What is the issue, and from this issue what needs to be done? People will discuss both points exhaustively but the very discussion is commonly a bypass, particularly if preconceptions are challenged or if galling commitments are dictated. The racial "problem" remains a problem simply because there is operating within it a variety of bias which exhibits itself in different frames of reference, different representations of personal and special interests, different manifestations of ignorance and isolation. The issue, therefore, is rarely met as a human problem. One person will focus upon present progress in race relations as satisfactory, because he remembers vividly the awful stagnation of fifty years ago. Another person will work in service of the Negro, while preserving an unconscious paternalism, like a mother treating an unwanted child. Another will allocate justice as he would distribute food in a disaster area, but with many motives other than justice. Another will live the anonymous life of normality, only to feel profound disturbance when the racial issue grates upon self, home, business, or locale.

It has been said, with a great deal of accuracy, that people think what they need. Opinions, attitudes, and beliefs usually change only when people are forced into new group loyalties that overpower their old ones. This process can occur when the validity of present needs is challenged by proving them to be spurious or secondary, with a concurrent illustration of true human needs. Fear of the Negro is not a human need, nor is the Negro at the lowest rung of the social ladder, nor is the black man needed as an extension of childhood fantasies. What is needed is a dynamic breakthrough in truth which will display racial injustice as costly, enervating, and insane, and which will illumine racism in terms of the terrible attrition that it exacts from both white and colored.

Whose is the authentic voice then, the one which has but one frame of reference, one valid view? Perhaps that voice which speaks from the experience of deprivation, that voice that can receive another like his own without adulterating its truth in a morass of subjectivism, or that voice which so understands Christianity that it can speak accurately for the agony of all men. The Negro voice, then—or its equivalent—a prophetic voice which speaks in bold terms of diagnosis and therapy. The issue is our treatment of the Negro, and the therapy is our treatment of him. He is the best judge of perspective and urgency in the present struggle, because his rights are the pawn, and because any debate of his rights, however necessary, well meaning, and intelligent, must be recognized as an act of impertinence toward him, like debating the pros and cons of allowing a man to choose his religion or to live with his wife. When we speak of objectivity in civil rights we must maintain the heavy obligation of growing to the human view, with its implication of cleaving through the emotive rhetoric and casting aside the side issues as irrelevant. And it seems to me that we will gain this priceless and ennobling view from no better source than from one who cannot afford to speak with anything less than experiential authority, from one whose cause would be irrevocably crippled by the slightest intimation of falsehood or exaggeration. To me this is powerfully demonstrated by the attitude of whites toward Adam Clayton Powell. They are correct in concluding that he has been "bought off," not by white interests, but by his ambition and instability, while posing as a spokesman for his people and a partner to their condition.

What the Negro has to say to us will be determined both by what we are and what we have made him—another way of asserting that the Negro is what he is because of what we insist on his being. He is saying to us that our general pose of superiority has cheapened and degraded us, and to such an extent that it is an open question as to just who is inferior. He is saying to us that people, any people, no longer concern us to any great degree—only the aura of respectability, power, glibness, and distraction that they can offer us. He is saying that one of the by-products of our expensive fixation upon race is a base seduction by things, to which we have willingly acceded to fill the unrestful vacuum where human values should be. He is saying that a painful and realistic distinction must be made between pure Christianity and what we practice, because they are not the same thing. He is saying that we are precariously finding reality both boring and fearful, and that we are now focused upon a host of illusions, since they alone are capable of tempting our jaded interest. He is saying that our fears are really not different from those we possessed as children, and that our values have kept a perfect pace with our fears. He is saying that the staging of white supremacy—all the costumes and posturing of 350 years—was child's play, and the play of very vicious children indeed, but that today's world cannot afford such brutal sport. He is saying that the blessed time in history has come wherein he is strong enough to check our personal ruin, and that the fight is not so much for his freedom as for ours.

There is no denying it, the Negro through the years has seen us precisely as we are—discrimination could not help but clarify the difference between what he saw and what we believed ourselves to be. Negro women have cared for white children and have known them to be as helpless as any. Negro boys have played with white youths in little Southern towns and in Northern slums, only to see a certain age breed the superman and the inferior. Negro athletes have seen the bars of inferiority drop in competition, and they will never again take seriously the superiority of the white man. Negroes in Harlem know too well the "supremacy" of the slumlord, the "numbers" man, and the retailer—they know it to be a supremacy of power, greed, and debasing immorality. Negro women have wondered at the shameful and mysterious promptings of guilt that have led white men to seek them out, as though the only way to atone for the parody of racial purity would be the wheedlings and rapes of furtive miscegenation. Negroes of all ages and classes have stood aghast at the astounding spectacle of white Christians, who would espouse a God Who was also an outcast Jew, while daring to decide who it was that Christ had given this world to, who it was that He had decided to save. We may wonder why the best satire of our time has not come from Negro pens, for material abounds on every side. It may be that we will still have such satire, when the deadly seriousness of present tensions will have eased, when the luxury of humor is once more possible, when the white is better able to bear the sight of himself.

Yet, while the Negro stands in perplexity and chagrin at the inconsistency of the white man-child who rules his world, the brutal and unpredictable debate of his destiny goes on in the forums and homes of the land. Mostly the debate is marked by a painlessness of solution; mostly, it is indicative of arrogance and naïveté; mostly, it is distinguished by the immaturity of paternalism, and by a power which refuses to hold itself responsible. Thus it is that the Negro's need for better housing is sometimes admitted, but not the Negro's right to live where he can. Negro unemployment is a concern, but not to the point of providing for economic redress. Negro education may be a problem, but not so much of a problem that it could threaten the dependency relationship of white parents and their children. Negro social mixing might be winked at, but not to such a degree that the shibboleth of private property be impugned. The white conflict springs from a racist complex that has long been an unmentionable yet deeply radical premise of our culture: The white world will use but will never accept the Negro, and that it will face itself only in versions of the *status quo* or, preferably, in the greedy search for continued white enhancement.

No real breakthrough is yet in evidence. Segregation might be depicted as a monster in its death throes, but so far, the dying monster is still extremely active. Desegregation might be fairly common, but integration is all areas of American life is hardly begun. This is simply because racial ostracism is self-sustaining and self-perpetuating, and its pattern goes something like this. Among Negroes, poverty is a majority situation which so restricts social mobility that the housing ghetto becomes inevitable; inferior housing breeds education of roughly the same quality as the housing that it serves; poor education anticipates the limitation of job opportunity; unemployment or underemployment breeds and supports poverty; poverty is the main undergirding of the slum, and then, the circle begins again. Meanwhile, to add to the complexity of the reality is the social disease of racism, which has its own virulent permanence, since it is both aware of the self-sustaining dynamism of segregation, and insists on it. As long as race is a factor, it is impossible to speak of mere poverty, slums, undergrade education, unemployment, etc.—they become, rather, Negro poverty, Negro slums, Negro education, and Negro unemployment. And as such they are an entirely different matter.

Is education the answer? Some are very didactic in saying that it is, while forgetting that a simplicist solution can hardly be expected to eradicate an evil which was three centuries in establishing itself, and which has now permeated the fiber of American life. Moreover, in these quarters where education is offered as a remedy, it is proposed as Negro education, whereas the need for it is total. Though white education is not as deprived as the Negro's in cultural and scientific content, it is more deprived in its morality, at least in those central aspects of morality which deal with human relationships. It is precisely here that the brutalizing force of segregation strikes the white—he is dehumanized by the unilateral decision to live in moral and social isolation from the largest American minority, and, more widely, from the majority of the human race. Under these conditions, the fearful attrition of asking the white to confront his vain and childish gestures of superiority is indeed a heavy price, but it is a necessary one. Without it, education needs a redefinition, because it has too little to say of the business of life.

Is the answer a war on poverty, even a program infinitely more ambitious than the one suggested by the President? To my mind, it is a dangerously naïve hypothesis to argue that under present conditions of moral immaturity, American whites will meet the actuality of poverty among Negroes, and this having been done, will accept that race once the Negro proletariat has disappeared. I say "naïve" because the Negro "presence" in America begins first in white minds, and Negro poverty is no more than a tangibly projected state of the poverty of white mentality, which expresses itself mostly through a bourgeois set of parochial and selfish attitudes. It is possible to assume that Christ's assertion of the perennial reality of the poor has been often taken to justify poverty and even to cause people to be poor, since the unpoor have traded their potential of inner wealth for material substance. Though, ideally speaking, it may be so that we now have the national resources to eliminate poverty, it is hard to see how this could happen, short of a greater moral commitment on the part of all Americans.

What then is the answer? Certainly, an assault upon poverty in all its ramifications, through a universal evaluation and upgrading of education, including the moral instruction on race that the churches so often neglect. Certainly, the creation of jobs, better security for the unemployed and aged and a more responsible approach to automation by industry. Certainly, a concerted national move to break up the racial ghetto, both through the integration of white housing, and by efforts to inspire whites to return to Negro areas in a spirit of fraternity and service.

But where will initiative for all of this come from? What will be the source of unanimity among Americans which will agree about what needs to be done as well as how it needs to be done? The impetus will be moral or it will fail miserably, both in terms of issue and urgency. The scope of our approach will be fraternal, or we will harvest such a crop of fratricide and social rupture that what we formerly knew as morality might become coercion by the state, imposed as a simple fact of existence. Gunnar Myrdal speaks of the inhibitions of Americans regarding public expenditure and state interference. This state is at least partly due to the moral inhibitions that plague us. They operate in the name of freedom, and for the objective of freedom, yet paradoxically make us victims of various currents of fear, guilt, and insecurity. We become men who remain free only in adding to our own slavery.

After all, under analysis, what can be said of a rationale which denounced the Negro as sub-human, which insists on a sub-human status for him, which manipulates society to keep him sub-human, and then judges him according to human standards? What can be said of the standards or of the humanity that produces them? One can only conclude that such criteria come from gravely sick people, whose illness is made somewhat inviolable by the fact that it goes unrecognized. What is behind such paranoia? Are not the claims of Negroes the claims of mere persons who are asking for what Christianity and our Constitution has long pledged them? If this is so, then why the outrage and fear? Is it because we are afraid to affirm upon the altar of ourselves that the Negro is a person like us? In our better moments, we must suspect that hair and features and skin color have nothing to do with being a person, even if we were to attempt the impossible task of proving that ours were better. Nor do they have anything to do with the unity of human nature nor redemption in Christ nor sonship in God. Is there, then, something deeper at work? Are we reluctant to receive the Negro as a person because this would inevitably and painfully mean that we would have to accept ourselves, face ourselves, *see* ourselves as the kind of persons that we are? What are we shielding in ourselves that we fear more than him? Is he a personification of the dark and terrible images that people our unconscious? Do we suspect that our vaunted superiority is a figment that will wither under exposure, like some lush parasitic plant that thrives under cover and dies in the sun? Would acceptance of him mean the banishment of a series of myths upon which our lives are often based, and which we hug under stress as a child hugs his doll in the dark? It may be that the securities of race, nationality, private property, and selective association which we trust so profoundly are not securities at all, but rather temerarious risks which stunt our humanity and close us to the world. It may be that these items of safeguard are in reality substitutions for persons and personal relationships that now occupy the central focus in our lives, having imposed a control upon us that is neither ours nor God's. It may be that the web of impregnability that we weave around ourselves has truly trapped us, for in keeping the Negro at the walls, we keep ourselves within—we have destroyed the capability of dealing with him or ourselves.

America is, I think, afraid of more than Negroes freed from their past and secure in the assets of full citizenship. We are, I suspect, very much afraid of the freedom that would come from giving the Negro his freedom, for in the course of achieving this reality, and later, keeping it real, we would have to lend our shoulders to the duties of mature men. Freedom for the Negro and maturity for us are reciprocal endowments—one calls for the other, one causes the other, one owes itself to the other. Does the adolescent fear manhood, or what manhood means? Do we fear maturity or the Negro—freedom for ourselves or his freedom?

Generally, however, Americans will not dare to deny that

the Negro is a person. What they *will* deny is the consistency that must flow from this premise. It is this lack of consistency that has produced our dilemma. Sydney Harris, an editorial columnist of *The Chicago Daily News*, wrote this statement:

> Either the Negro is a full-fledged human being, and a complete American citizen, or he is less than a human being and incapable of citizenship. If we believe the first, the Negro must be assured of all his civil and legal and human rights. If we believe the second, the Negro must be stripped of citizenship and made a ward of the state. No middle course is possible. Most Americans, on both sides of the issue, refuse to face this central point. The Negro should be treated just like everyone else—no better, no worse—or else he should be confined to a reservation, returned to Africa, or sent back into slavery. Any other solution is just hypocrisy and foolishness, and only postpones the ultimate day of reckoning. Is the Negro a man, or is he not a man? Once we answer this question honestly, all the other answers fall into place, painfully but surely. I happen to believe that he is a man (though grievously flawed by centuries of abuse), created by the same God that created the rest of us. To treat him any differently is, to my mind, an act of profound impiety. Those who think otherwise should not make any concessions they do not believe in. They should not hide behind the deception of "separate but equal" schools or any other such mumbo-jumbo. They should frankly ask that the Negro be assigned to a sub-human status in our society. If we do not think that the Negro is a man, we should both ignore his "rights" and absolve his "responsibilities." If he cannot live anywhere, work anywhere, eat anywhere, go to school anywhere, then he should not be asked to pay taxes, to fight for his country, to give his time, his labor, or his loyalty to enterprises in

which he cannot share. The white man has made the Negro what he is, and has kept him where he is. Nobody knows how far the Negro can go up, because he has never had the chance; we only know how far he can go down—and it frightens us terribly—because we have pushed him down. We have refused to let him live decently, and then we accuse him of the sin of indecency. So we think the Negro is a man or not a man? We can no longer squirm and back away from this crucial question. For already having postponed it so long, either answer that we decide upon will bring anguish to millions.*

In refusing the corollaries of his humanity, in every meaning that it has or could have, we punish ourselves terribly. In fact, the mania of our refusal, by its very inaccuracy, illustrates to a frightening degree the dimensions of our moral mutilation. In other words, if we want a yardstick of what we are, individually and collectively, our view of the Negro is that yardstick. We are, to an astounding degree, what we think him to be, what we are prepared to do for him, what we will allow him to do for us. Thomas Merton speaks of white and Negro being co-relative to each other, and he maintains that reciprocity in this case is a providential relationship. He says further that "white is for black and black is for white." It is worth commenting that when white is for white and black is for neither because he cannot be otherwise as things are, then self-destruction is the rule. Self-destruction in us that takes the form of an illusory position with psychotic overtones—buried fears, self-deception, and latent viciousness. Self-destruction in the Negro—schizophrenia, introjected hate and dull, pointless despair. And since the Negro knows precisely what the white state of mind is, being forced to live it as well as by it, his appeal to us takes on the nature of a proph-

* Sydney Harris, *Chicago Daily News.*

ecy, and we can say without exaggeration or overblown idealism that God is using him to speak to us about ourselves in
this country in much the same sense that God is using Communism to speak to us in the world.

III

The connection of segregation with a world arms race is by
no means an imaginative one. To the ordinary American, the
Negro is an unknown quantity, who inexplicably has taken
upon himself a course of action which threatens to expose
white supremacy, its myths and virulence, in the full light of
day. Practically speaking, we think that we have solved the
threat of the Negro; our attempted solution consists in a wide
variety of moves designed to keep him from thinking that he
is other than the inferior being, genetically and culturally,
that we have decided him to be. Taking this as sort of a
national climate of decision on one great issue, what reaction
can we look for when the international threat of the Communist looms on our horizon? Can we be expected to react according to a larger imagination or breath of mind? The
Communist threat is still a relatively new phenomenon to us
and, therefore, still laden with anxiety, still unpredictable in
its course. But it is essentially of the same nature as the Negro
threat. Both Negro and Communist challenge directly and
aggressively our assumed identity, what we believe ourselves
to be, what we wishfully think of ourselves. On the one hand,
we have nativist supremacy associated with a white skin to
inflate our ego; on the other, the engrafted supremacy spring-
ing from a superior ethos, a superior way of life, superior
wealth, and so on. And consequent to this pride, an international transference of policy and attitude occurs, a policy
with the same psychosis as the one employed so widely and
effectively at home. Very shortly, we have internationalized
our attitudes of injustice and exclusivism, our determination

to preserve our status quo of privilege and possession. And this to such an extent that we are still creeping toward that apex of irresponsibility in which nuclear war appears more and more logical as the bold sanction of our national integrity. We find ourselves caught in a position which Archibald Mac-Leish concisely describes as "knowing as a mind what we cannot comprehend as a man." We know precisely what we are doing to the Negro, and we know what we are capable of doing to the Communists, but a comprehension of the real or possible effects of our action is beyond us.

This opacity of outlook is not to be wondered at. The national self-education, consequent to our treatment of Negro citizens, has prepared us for a closed international life, profoundly suspicious and unimaginative. We turn away, with undisguised aversion from the misery of our own citizens, with a feeling of querulous injury that their sufferings should pierce the inviolability of our sensual and dreamlike existence. Such morality is ripe for enlargement; so we see neither paradox or contradiction in building the same weapons force that the Russians build, making like promises, issuing like threats, wooing the same friends with the same bribes, and reacting with profound irritability at any hint of the need of re-evaluation, or the possibility that our course may be less than ideally right. The national reaction to the speech of Senator William Fulbright on the need for thinking the "unthinkable" on foreign policy studiously reveals our position.

In a more subdued tone, U Thant has remarked that both Russia and the United States misunderstand their roles in history. Both, he said, are victims of their past. Russia has an obsessive fear of encirclement, rooted in her memories of 1919, when foreign troops, including those of the United States, invaded her soil to intervene on behalf of the anti-Bolshevik forces. And as for the U.S., we were rudely dragged to the center of the world stage by the unprovoked attack on

Pearl Harbor. Thant says: "The fear that such a catastrophic surprise attack will be repeated dominates the thinking of Washington."*

To exemplify the extent of this thinking, we note the talent hunt for scientific intellectuals by the government through the military-industrial complex of the nation. In spite of individual moral scruples, group purposes do not encourage these men to view their professional life in moral terms, to deal with others as individuals, or to work in a way which is critical or open to flexibility and new methods of exploring peace. Rather, as one commentator put it: "Scientists in government service are symbols of a system whose two key words are not life or death, but Communism and anti-Communism."† Now, it is agreed by thinking men that both the sciences and the arts are transcendent in their source and application, and that a consequent moral duty attends their use. The dereliction of this duty results in bad science or bad art, for in both cases the purification and enhancement of human life is lost as an objective. This general reflection seems of point here. As Harold Taylor, chairman of the Committee on Peace Research, says: "The universities, including their scientific faculties, once were the major counterforce to naked power and material values. But they themselves have been seduced by a mixture of money and invitations to patriotic duty until research budgets for studies of weapons systems, military research, cold-war politics, and industrial development occupy major research facilities in this country's institutions."**

The reliance that we have placed on extermination weapons since Dresden and Tokyo, since Hiroshima and Nagasaki, has encouraged an unhealthy national trust in the military status quo, through which crucial moral decisions are made by a

* U Thant, *Progressive*, May, 1962.
† Dr. James McDonald, *Progressive*, May, 1962.
** Harold Taylor, *Progressive*, May, 1962.

small and powerful military group, without benefit (as far as we know) of informed or expert moral opinion. In such a way we risk enthroning military procedures as an absolute; and we support such procedures, unchallenged and beyond criticism, by unlimited university and industrial research, by vast expenditures of money, and a public opinon which is both emotional and unthinking. In this regard, the farewell address of former President Dwight D. Eisenhower to the nation is deserving of sober thought:

> We have been compelled to create a permanent armaments industry of vast proportions. Added to this, three and a half million men and women are directly engaged in the defense establishment. We annually spend on military security alone more than the net income of all United States corporations.
>
> Now, this conjunction of an immense military establishment and a large arms industry is new in the American experience. The total influence—economic, political, even spiritual—is felt in every city, every state house, every office of the Federal government. We recognize the imperative need for this development. Yet we must not fail to comprehend its grave implications. Our toil, resources, and livelihood are all involved; so is the very structure of our society.
>
> In the councils of government, we must guard against the acquisition of unwarranted influence, whether sought or unsought, by the military-industrial complex. The potential for the disastrous rise of misplaced power exists and will persist.

To admit all this is, of course, another thing than a fatalistic admission that even now the cause of peace is in complete jeopardy. The very opposite is true; and suggestions are at hand for an imaginative, bold use of our resources in the continuing struggle for man's future. In place of unchallenged military spending and research, it has been advised that the Federal government sponsor university research for the foundation of peace strategy. Such research would be aimed at acquainting our people with the truth of the world situation, and at providing our diplomats with fresh and pertinent ideas with which to judge and exercise leadership in history. One thinks of the contribution to peace of a world university, with exchange professors and students drawn from all the nations of the world, offering a curriculum of world problems, beginning with those of war and the causes of war. Such an institution, ideally, would graduate men dedicated to their world, free of the parochialism of the nation-state and from slavery to national interests. Another possibility suggests that we enlarge the present sharing of scientific information and cooperation in scientific projects. There is also the value of easing trade and travel restrictions; of withdrawing troops from some of the nations which encircle Russia, and generally of reducing our nuclear components overseas; of working more actively to strenghten the United Nations; of studying and implementing the proposals of Pius XII's 1939 and 1940 Christmas messages and of Pope John's *Mater et Magistra* and *Pacem in Terris*. In sum, as Catholics and as Americans, we must react with instant and immediate rebellion against fatalism and selfish, insular thinking, which far more symptomatic of a paranoiac dream world than of a virile understanding of patriotism, human solidarity, or religious life.

And as a new way of regarding man and his world, Albert Einstein seemed to sense our impasse years ago. He said: "Our world is threatened by a crisis whose extent seems to escape those within whose power it is to make major decisions for good or evil. The unleashed power of the atom has changed everything except our ways of thinking. Thus we are drifting toward a catastrophe beyond comparison. We shall require a substantially new manner of thinking if mankind is to survive."

And in the wings, but still controlling the stage, is the unspeakable, horror-laden threat of the bomb. Bill Mauldin, in a cartoon in *The St. Louis Post-Dispatch*, depicted our country and Russia as two superbombs, worriedly observing the scurryings of a group of vicious, parasitic little bombs about them. These latter are the new, cheap, simple nuclear weapons. The cartoon is captioned "Population Explosion." There is not fantasy here. The major parasites are proliferating their own spawn and the only thing to be answered is the flat, military question of how cheap such weapons are. Certainly they would not be cheap if they were ever used. But bombs for ICBM's, of the conventional type borne by the Strategic Air Command, bombs for Polaris missiles, for artillery and mortar shells, for the numerous variety of Army and Air Force short- and intermediate-range missiles—these are another matter indeed. Some Americans are doubtlessly worried because the Army has not yet announced that it has perfected bombs for hand-grenade and small-arms use. So goes the thinking; unawakened, childishly optimistic, mischievously at distance from reality.

What we have not visualized to any noticeable degree is what would happen to an area in case of nuclear attack from abroad. Dr. James E. McDonald,* of the Institute of Atmospheric Physics at the University of Arizona, has described the probable effects on his state, if two twenty-megaton bombs were exploded near the earth surface, one at Tucson, another at Phoenix. Each bomb would equal the explosive force of 20 million tons of TNT.

The fission products produced by the explosion would reach multimillion degree heat a fraction of a second after detonation, creating incandescent gases and a shock wave.

* Dr. James E. McDonald, *Progressive*, May, 1962.

The fireball would expand to a diameter of 2 miles in ten seconds, and the mushroom cloud would blossom to an altitude of 17 miles or more. Beneath, a crater 3,000 feet deep and 3,500 feet in diameter would be scooped from the earth. The shock wave would move out at a speed exceeding 750 miles per hour—in less than half a minute, 90 per cent of Tucson would be homeless. Within 8 miles from ground zero, trucks and automobiles would be rolled along the ground and into other objects. Ninety per cent of the trees would be uprooted within the same radius, utility poles would be snapped and debris of all description would block every road and street. In the twenty seconds following explosion, there would be flash burning of skin and the ignition of all flammable objects, including clothing. Deciduous leaves would burn within a radius of 2 miles, the nearby mountains would be solid banks of flaming vegetation. There would be neither water nor personnel to fight the fires. Fallout would be concentrated locally, but would also extend in lethal doses to an area of 2,000 to 20,000 miles downwind. Shock, attacking the survivors within fifteen to twenty minutes after detonation, would prevent them from initiating intelligent flight. Even a momentary glance at the fireball would cause temporary or permanent blindness, and the so-called fire storms, of the kind which followed the British and American saturation bombing of World War II in several German cities, could be expected; killing by suffocation, sucking people on the periphery of the blast area into the holocaust, and making first- and second-degree burns the most serious medical problem of the area.

How much warning would there be? By estimation, Tucson is fifteen minutes by intercontinental missile from Anadyr Peninsula in Siberia. The Kennedy Administration admitted, in its booklet "Fallout Protection," that "enemy missiles could arrive unannounced." If they were fired from enemy submarine, there might be no warning at all. We must visualize, therefore, the hysteria of populations in flight, the panic at the scene of the explosion, the shock of the sight of those struck by radiation, the tragedy of people calling for doctors who are themselves already dead or injured. And this is only the beginning—the first hour. In the next days, the so-called "normal" illnesses would take hold; the virus infections, typhoid fever, and amoebic dysentery would strike as immunity became notably reduced. The shelter dweller (the American people have made an almost wholesale rejection of shelters) must think of how he will obtain food and water when he comes out. If his home has collapsed over him, he must wait until the radiation danger decreases, hoping that he can get out or be dug out.

No expert has yet completely synthesized all the hazards of nuclear war. Up to the present time only one effect has been studied—radiation; so the gross effects of nuclear explosion, as it is known to our people, is much less gory than a complete picture would show. But to give a realistic and accurate idea of the conditions in a given area as a result of such an explosion is an impossible task. It eclipses the imagination and defies the mind's powers. At any rate, such a description has never been attempted, in an obvious effort to "harden the American will." And thus, many vital questions are passed over. What, for example, do men do upon emerging from their shelter, supposing that they had fled safely to one, and supposing it has succeeded in saving its occupants? What of food, water, medical attention, decontamination of the atmosphere? The full question of the dangers of such an attack has been treated with a kind of deliberately induced Madison Avenue fog. Only the less unfavorable points have been stressed; the more unfavorable ones are buried or camouflaged. And the graphs which abound to chart the recovery of the nation manage to be both neat and outrageously misleading. Dr. Herman Kahn, in one of these, presents this series of conjectures: if 2 million

American citizens are killed in the war, the nation will be back on its feet in a year; if 20 million are killed, it will take ten years; 80 million, a half century; 160 million, a full century. Such formulas do not deserve intelligent consideration.

It is unequivocal and accurately blunt statements by our leaders that we need, including those of the Church. And we need to hear them often enough to allow them to penetrate the mind and to shock us from our deadly and irrational lethargy. Pius XII, as early as 1943, condemned "total war," and called it an "apocalyptic monster"; and yet many disciples of the "morality" of our present stance will insanely deny that nuclear war need necessarily be total. Again in 1943, he called World War II a "war of aggression," implying that neither side could defend their stand as being moral. In 1944, he called for "war on war," and asserted that we have a moral obligation "to ban all wars of aggression," a duty which "brooks no delay, no procrastination, no hesitation, no subterfuge." In 1954, he called ABC warfare a "sin, an offense, and an outrage against the majesty of God." Jules Cardinal Saliege asks this in the same vein: "Are we drunk, or are we insane? We are using our power in order to destroy. Ten million men were killed in the first world war, 40 million in the second; if a third war comes, there is every indication that far more than a hundred million will die. You can truthfully say that the devil is calling the tune . . . God did not create the world in order that it might be made into a hell. God did not create man to be a permanent murderer."* The French bishops in 1950 said abruptly and decisively: "We condemn nuclear weapons with all our strength." Pope John of blessed memory, in his encyclical *Pacem in Terris*, maintains that "justice, right reason and humanity, therefore, urgently demand that the arms race should cease; that the stockpiles that exist in several countries should be reduced equally and simultane-

---

* Jules Cardinal Saliege, Pastoral Letter, 1949.

ously by the parties concerned; that nuclear weapons should be banned; and that a general agreement should eventually be reached about progressive disarmament and effective methods of control." Finally, our most respected military men join in warning us of our terrible peril. General Douglas MacArthur said: "War has become a Frankenstein to destroy both sides. No longer does it possess the chance of the winner of the duel—it contains, rather, the germs of double suicide." And General H. H. Arnold repeated this with his own emphasis: "One nation cannot defeat another nation today. That concept died at Hiroshima."

And so we have it. A dilemma is thrust upon us by God, mankind, and history. Thomas Merton speaks of the corruption of the moral sense that afflicts our nation. And his charge cannot be lightly dismissed, when Americans, in fact, contemplate the misery of some 10 percent of their population without serious moral unease. His charge gains immeasurable validity when we become aware that Americans can debate, peacefully, measures which could lead to the slaughter of a million of our own citizens, and a comparable or greater number of Europeans and Asians. To show the quality of our ironically sick humor, we find ourselves lamenting in public that the growth of biological knowledge has not kept pace with our progress in atomic physics. In consequence, we must go slow on advocating deterrent nuclear war, since we do not yet have the means to repair its human ruin. We can jocularly speculate, as has been said, with a tinge of bitter irony, that God could solve the race question by merely changing all men black and all women white, or vice versa, and then let biology take its course. Or we can suggest that the vacation-bound American merely tow his air-raid shelter behind his car. Or we can cling to a suggestion that was made in serious vein by another "student" of the nuclear sport. When international tension makes war seem imminent, he said, all the relevant data of weapons systems of both sides should be fed into computers, so that a simulated war might be fought with international referees, a chessboard victor being declared by the computers. This, he suggested, would provide a release for both sides, would forestall the necessity of killing millions of people, and at the same time, would give the politicians and militarists the games they seemed determined to play. But these are clever, irrelevant games, and we can dismiss them as soon as we have laughed at them.

But the predicament remains. It is far more pertinent for us of the Church to understand our responsibility to the questions of segregation and the arms race, for it is becoming increasingly apparent that more than ever before in history the Church is emerging as the spiritual and social hope of mankind. We believe that Christ came to restore creation to His Father. We are convinced, as Pope John was, that He is the only source of peace. We know that we will liberate the Divine Action in the world only by living Christ's function of Priesthood and Prophecy. We know that without the light of Christ aflame in Christian hearts, men will seek a false redemption in the world, or will continue to build up present progressive tensions until, by the very nature of things, the situation will erupt in appalling destruction. If we see all of these truths in a living way we will be aware of the scope of our duty.

IV

But there are formidable obstacles to a viable understanding of this. In his *Lay People in the Church*, Fr. Yves Congar, by way of example, emphasizes the dangerous lack of attention given to secondary causes in Pre- and Post-Reformation theology. He suggests that in these periods, the clergy were occupied almost exclusively with primary causes, the absolutes of the sacral order, and that laymen were delegated to the secular order by forfeit, since "they were left to live in the world to be a part of it, but nothing more." Nor were the absolutes or sacred resources of the Church given to the layman in such a way that he could apply them as means to organize and sanctify society. As a result of this condition, perduring over several centuries, the balance and unity between the hierarchy and the laity was weakened, and for practical purposes, in many parts of Europe, the Church became a priesthood without a laity. It was this situation, with all its implications, that the Reformers attacked in the sixteenth century. For example, Luther said: "Christ has not got two bodies, nor two kinds of body, the one spiritual and the other temporal." And the result of the reform action was the establishment of a laity without a priesthood. It was fairly predictable, then, what direction the Catholic Counter-Reformation would take; it would fight for the things threatened by Luther and Calvin; it would emphasize the primacy of the hierarchy in the Church. Though Trent would make some provision for the laity, the Church continued to view them, by and large, as passive recipients of clerical ministrations, rather than as members of a Body performing an indispensable temporal function in the world of man as a sacred consequence of their faith.

Our theology is only beginning to recover balance. Through the influence that the Scriptural and Liturgical revivals are having, theology is beginning again to consider seriously the secondary causes: people and things, events, technology, culture, history, and the stuff of society. Michael de la Bedoyere has a good proposition to advance in this regard. He says that no solutions to the world's problems can be deduced immediately from Christian dogma. The conscience of lay Christians must mediate between dogma and effective action; that is, action directed intelligently toward precise conditions of time and place. But unless the consciences of laymen are both capable and ready to implement the generalities of dogma in a particular context, no action of a thoughtful and effective kind will ensue. Our historic failure, therefore, lies basically with our theology, which for long has had a tendency to become inbred and overspeculative. Consequently, one notices the common attitude toward the Church and toward society which Daniel-Rops compares to the attitude of a Frenchman to his country: "France begets us, we do not beget her." Frenchmen often regard their country as a gift given once and for all, something they have received without the obligation of constructive action on her behalf. And so it is with Christians. Neither the laity, nor to a notable degree, the clergy, have deeply absorbed the public consequences of the Mystical Body; so they find it difficult to make the hurdle from dogma to the Negro, to the arms race, to a generally accepted international mind.

In terms of need, we have learned neither the scope nor the depth of the Redemption; hence, we cannot see that a Christian solution to the nuclear dilemma is both possible in principle and expedient in fact. We do not sufficiently understand the Eucharist as Sacrifice and as Sacrament, so we fail to realize the consequence that a community is fed spiritually through the Christians within it, in such a way that all men are supported by the interest, concern, and active love of those who partake of a Body of sacrificial love.

What suggestions then? The sober drum of statistics, the repetitious analyses of conditions, the flights in idealism—all these come to very little, apart from the will to follow through into perceptive and concerted action. First, there is the matter of conviction. An extremely wise and informed French journalist, who knows the Western Church with insight and objectivity, once said to me: "You American Catholics are today the measure of the Church." And perhaps an analogy can be drawn from the way he developed his theme.

We must be to the Church what our country must be to the world. Doesn't such a statement merely borrow, in more particular terms, Cardinal John Henry Newman's idea? "In all times," he said, "the laity have been the measure of the Christian spirit; they saved the Irish Church, and they betrayed the Church in England." But to contrast the talent of the laity in the United States, its unlimited potential in vocations to the Religious and lay life, its uncluttered history, is freedom from anti-clericalism and political ideology—to contrast all these with what the laity has accomplished is to demonstrate what our laity are equipped to do here and now.

Then, too, there is the matter of experience. The ordinary Christian life is not presently oriented to the crucial concerns of human experience—the winning and preservation of peace, the elimination of racial and religious discrimination, the proposed assault upon poverty, the appraisal of the nation-state concept. We must remove whatever it is that insulates us from contact with these problems, since the future of mankind will depend upon the course that they take. The Christian, therefore, must open himself to an education by these profound and momentous movements, for they can express to him a ministry of experience, even as they look to him for a ministry of direction. In this way, the dialectic between theology and life is maintained, a reciprocal influence is established—the Christian returns to his theology to speak to it of life, and returns to life to speak to it of theology.

The words of Feodor Dostoyevsky are perhaps more relevant today than when he wrote them. "He who turns away from mankind," he said, "is an atheist." Mankind pleads today for the Christ Whom we alone can give; men beg wordlessly for our talent of mind and strength of body, for our view of the universe, for the courage with which we confront history, for the view of the Church which regards her as the mother of nations, for our transcendence of principle and immanence of action, for our presence and ministry. In our generation, it is finally true that the world belongs to those who love it most. And only three eventualities can possibly spring from the refusal or acceptance of such a view of things: The world will be saved by us for God, or it will go by default to those who love it for its own sake, or the selfishness of the West and the zeal of the East will rise to a collaborative zenith of utter destruction. In such a way, it becomes clear that the world literally waits upon the decision of Christians to love, to serve, to save.

6. Race and the Christian Conscience

It is inevitable that a certain measure of incongruity creep into the present situation of race relations in the United States, since large numbers of Americans are unaware of the irony and embarrassment of their position. In this regard, the story is told of a high official of our government who had just witnessed the formal birth of one of the new African nations. After the ceremonies, when the parades and speeches had ended and the new flag fluttered proudly above his head, our American official turned to a large colored man standing next to him, threw his arms about him, and exclaimed: "Brother, aren't you happy to be free?" The Negro was frankly perplexed and answered: "Sir, I'm on your staff." And then, thinking that something more was required of him, he added: "I don't know about things like freedom. I'm from Alabama."

Roughly, there are two different types of audience that any writer envisions in dealing with this subject. One is made up of people of good will and remarkable resources of charity; another is burdened with rationalized guilt, a variety of inaccurate knowledge, folklore, and emotional problems that in areas of race relations could only be called illness. In speaking of race, an appeal must be made to these very different publics for different reasons and with the expectation of different results. Let me illustrate what I mean. Some time ago, in New Orleans, a young priest was sent to a "white" parish to offer two Masses on a Sunday. (In New Orleans, and in other cities of the Deep South, parishes are often distinguished as white or colored.) The Gospel of the Sunday spoke of the testing of

Our Lord by a Doctor of the Law; and from this encounter, the two great commandments of the Love were enunciated in a new setting. The priest came prepared to preach on this text with an application to the injustice of segregation. He quoted his text and the words of Christ: "On these two commandments depend the whole Law and the Prophets." He was getting nicely launched into his sermon when suddenly there came an abrupt disturbance from the congregation. A man was on his feet in the middle of the church, waving his arms excitedly and shouting toward the pulpit: "Hey! I didn't come here to listen to this junk. I came to hear Mass!" The priest stopped talking and waited quietly. His self-control made the parishioner even more provoked. He cried out again, adding that he would leave if the sermon were not terminated. Here and there, in the congregation, he won support. Another gentleman made himself heard, said that he would not endure such a sermon, emphasizing, too, that he would leave the church if the priest did not return to the altar. The priest still waited. Whereupon, the two men, followed by about fifty other Catholics, left amid confusion and acrid recrimination, the first gentleman administering the *coup de grâce* with a shout: "If I miss Mass today, you're responsible." The story seems to have point for several reasons; first, it illustrates the enormity of the crisis of conscience by Southern whites; secondly, it brings attention to the vacuum of teaching on the subject; thirdly, it insists that a courageous and unequivocal approach to this situation is essential if error is to be eradicated and truth implanted. For in the long run the majority of American Catholics will accept truth if it is properly presented. And the rest we must leave to Heaven.

Again, there are great advantages in bringing the subject of race, in season and out, before the consciences of our people. For just as there are degrees of prejudice, ranging from violent opposition to a rather flabby indifference, so also are there degrees of conviction. It is unquestionable that the greatest contributing factor to the painfully slow progress of race relations in this country is not the lack of governmental action, not the opposition of the Dixiecrats, not the racists so vociferous in both North and South, but the silence of the "moderates," those many good people who, in this issue, are frightfully inexperienced, ignorant, apprehensive, unconvinced, uncommitted, merely "good." One hopes, by courageous speech, to take a moderate or two off the fence. And along positive lines, one hopes to prepare Catholics for a more intense apostolate in this crucial area of human relations, in order that the vast numbers who are emotionally unready for the problem may be brought nearer its reality.

It grows clearer every day that try as we might, we cannot escape the Negro. Even the whites fleeing to suburbia in New York City, in Washington, in Philadelphia, Detroit, and Chicago find that they must take their consciences with them and that flight merely delays the inevitable. In this regard, one remembers the shouted words of the Secretary of State of Louisiana (everyone in the South except the Negro seems to shout when they speak on this issue) at a White Citizens Councils' meeting: "All them Yankees can run outa New York to the Island or up the river, or they can run outa Washington to Maryland or Virginia, but where we gonna run, inta the Gulf of Mexico? Ah'm gonna stay and fight." These attitudes, flight or fight, are questionable, but which of the two, we might ask ourselves, is the more honest?

To come nearer the issue, a story comes to mind which exemplifies the typical American attitude toward what we might term with more precision the white problem of conscience. A sociologist happened to be visiting an art museum in one of the cultural centers of the Old South. There he was particularly taken with a striking sculpture in terra-cotta called "Soldier in the Rain," a statue which really represented a colored man, lynched by hanging. The visitor was absorbed in admiring the statue with two elderly Southern ladies who were guiding him about the place. When he remarked to them that the statue was a most remarkable example of its subject, a lynched Negro, they became emotionally wrought, said that it was a simple portrayal of an executed soldier, and even brought forth newspaper clippings to prove their point. Rather wryly, the man countered with the fact that soldiers are never executed by hanging, either in war or during peace-time. At this, their disturbance became more apparent, and began to verge on anger. Seeing that the situation was worsening, the sociologist left them. But his curiosity was aroused, and he went to look for the artist, a man who lived and worked nearby. The artist, as the sociologist discovered, was a Latin American of almost purely Indian descent, and hence, of very dark skin. (His complexion sometimes made things acutely painful for him, as it had recently when he had been caught on the street with a white woman, and, unrecognized by the police, he had been given a severe beating.) The visitor opened the conversation by complimenting him on his work; he told him of his experience at the museum and finally asked him to clear up the matter of the subject of the sculpture. The artist casually remarked that there was nothing to clear up; his work was merely an abstract piece representing a soldier, "any soldier." The sociologist became exasperated at the continuing duplicity and heatedly insisted that the statue represented a lynched Negro. It was an odd situation, he went on, when a spectator had a deeper understanding of a piece of art than did its creator. This broke the resistance of the artist; he admitted frankly that he intended the statue to represent a lynched Negro. His answer perplexed the sociologist, and he asked: "Aren't you aware that everyone will know it for what it is?" "Yes, they'll know it," said the artist, "but they don't want to know it." "Then why did you make it? No one will dare to buy it, no one will dare to have it in their house?" "I know that," the poor man answered sadly, "I make it for myself and I'm going to put it in a closet. It shouldn't be called 'Soldier in the Rain,' but 'American Skeleton in the Closet.' It's the great deception between the public and myself."

The troubled sculptor is symbolic and even symptomatic of an American society troubled by the unwelcome presence of minority groups, and especially by the Negro. The principles which should control our attitudes are crystal clear and most emphatic. Our Christian heritage, the admirable provisions of our law, the tenacious adherence of all of us to what has been called the "Great American Experiment," all urge us in the same direction. For we believe, having ourselves been a part of the American process, that the success of our experiment depends on the fusion of all our people into a national whole, the acceptance of all presently here, and the assimilation of succeeding waves of immigration into the American mainstream. The principles are clear indeed, but in the case of the Negro, they are largely ineffectual. He is in our house, but he is in a closet, and we fear to bring him forth into polite company.

II

I think that our next step is to consider the temper of the average Southerner, because like most of us, he is largely a product of religious, social, and economic influences. I venture that we of the North, especially those of us who might possess strong moral convictions on the matter of race, or who might be merely unaffected by the problem, sin through oversimplification in regard to the Southerner. We tend to categorize his actions into areas of right or wrong, the thing to do or the thing not to do. By such summary judgment we reach conclusions that are often subjective, unrealistic, and highly offensive. The Northern press has especially sinned in this. Editorials and general news coverage since 1954 have been scathing and even hypocritical, betraying by a lack of sympathy and objectivity an intolerable ignorance of Southern history and customs. Naturally, the Southern press has sometimes replied in kind, sending its reporters to the North for ammunition, pointing to Harlem, the Black Belt of Chicago, the "inner cities" in a hundred Northern communities, the plight of Negro migrant workers who choose to remain in the North where they must undergo a new type of segregation. Northern tourists, too, have often generated more heat than light while in contact with their Southern neighbors; and many a Southerner still spits out the word "Yankee" with as much unspoken disgust and hidden animosity as in Civil War days or during the Reconstruction Period. We of the North often fall victim to a very human failing, pontificating from the ivory tower of untested moral conviction, of established patterns of law, and of security from a problem whose true complexity and presence we ourselves are at pains to avoid. We have generally been aghast at Little Rock, at the treatment given the Freedom Riders, at the fear and death in Oxford, at the murder of Medgar Evans and the four Birmingham children, at the "police state" atmosphere in Mississippi and Alabama. Yet we forget that the North also has a situation of explosive content, and that many Negroes have left the South only to encounter in the North a variety of discrimination as fully effective as the old experience. We forget that the old vicious circle of segregation still breeds hopelessness, inertia, irresponsibility, resentment, and even hatred. We forget that a tremendous national potential is never fully realized, that local communities suffer through a dry rot of complacency, that the Negro cannot contribute to the commonweal because he has so small a chance for a human life, and that our contribution is limited by the fact that we refuse to be human beings.

But to return to the Southerner. People below the Mason-Dixon line have always been, in a very true sense, something of a people within a people, and they have built there a country within a country. Their society has been typified by sociologists as aristocratic, class-conscious folk and closed—a situation quite phenomenal in the normal American picture. The French and Spanish left their mark in Southern Louisiana and the Spanish left theirs in Florida, but the greater part of this vast Southern area was settled by Anglo-Saxons, by pioneers from the Eastern colonies; by ex-indentured servants, who, having gained their freedom, moved West with the expectation of free land; by the descendants of the original penal colony of General James Ogelthorpe in Georgia. For the most part, these pioneers were English, Welsh, Scotch, and Protestant Irish. Imagine, then, a proud, highly individualistic and self-sufficient people, whose ancestors had fled Europe for much the same reason as the earlier Puritans, and who now left the coastal areas to seek a new beginning and a new land, in whose boundaries they could, above all, determine their own lives. They were tough and hardy, and they acclimated well to new conditions, heat and humidity, new soil, new food and crops. They were brave and reckless fighters, as witnessed by their contribution in the Revolutionary War and in the War of 1812, by their astounding struggle against the North, and by their work in settling the West. And yet, by a concatenation of circumstance and personal traits, every facet of their lives—religious, social, economic, and geographical—worked to make their society a closed one—personal, introverted, and quite effectively removed from outside influence.

First, we must mention the religion of the South. With rare exceptions (and these exceptions were far more influenced than influencing), the South's religion has been Fundamentalist, emphasizing a literal interpretation of the Bible, a Calvinist theology which interpreted material blessings as signs of Divine favor, a worship with pronounced stress on emotionalism. Southerners have long been known as the most religious people in our country; it is no accident that much of the intense religious culture of the Negro can be traced to their former masters. But what a religion! Its theology vague and unsystematized, morbidly concerned about sin, viewing Christ as an epiphany of the avenging Old Testament God, claiming no practical ethics, a religion that was a cathartic for inner turmoil, buried guilt, and personal frustration. It kept conscience salved by periodic encounters with the Spirit, convincing the person, beyond any reasonable doubt, that Jesus would "do all." The religious revivals that began in earnest about 1800 were orgiastic and tumultuous; they provided the people with an opportunity to meet and eat and court, and there is no evidence that the last was neglected.

The result of all this was a confused, emotionally charged, and sometimes violent approach to life and its problems. Far from interpreting life in terms of religious belief, the average Southerner often adapted (and still does) his religious belief to fit the framework of his life, and what he had decided life to be. Even when this became difficult, morality, though square, was made to fit, was torturously made to conform to prejudices. The class system, miscegenation before and after the Civil War, ruthless economics, slavery, refusal of suffrage for the Negro, politics, all became opportunities and occasions for the application of a situation ethics. In the mind of the Southerner, the question became reductively this: What morality will best serve the Way of Life decided upon as best for us? A Southerner, James McBride Dabbs, has remarked that the South has long been the most politically minded section of the country, because it "has had the impossible political job of keeping a changeless society in a changing world." Or as James Branch Cabell, another Southerner, put it: "Our actual tragedy is not that our fathers were badly treated, but that we ourselves are constitutionally unable to do anything except talk about how badly our fathers were treated." The "Southern Way of Life" is not a recent creation; it is the almost universal practical decision of the Southerner to preserve the status quo and resist with singular, and sometimes violent, energy any effort at change.

It would be quite unpardonable to overlook the enormous part played by slavery in forming the make-up of the Southerner. It is perhaps accurate to say that slavery provided the Southerners with, so to speak, a claim to fame; it was the only institution that would allow them to hold up their heads economically and obtain the status that Southerners so fiercely longed for in economic and national affairs. The South had no choice but to promote an agrarian economy, since land was her greatest resource, underpopulation a fact, and available labor her greatest need. Her large cities, even Atlanta, New Orleans, Richmond, and Natchez, were little more than overgrown rural centers. At the time of the Civil War, the North possessed 95 percent of the country's heavy industry; the South had but two foundries, one in Richmond, the other in New Orleans. The North claimed 75 percent of the nation's railroads and all of its locomotive shops. The South produced almost no coal, iron, or steel; she had no Navy and only 10 percent of the nation's shipping. But the South did have her rich coastal and delta lands, her "Black Wealth," as the Negroes were often called, her cotton, corn, tobacco, rice, indigo, and flax. All things considered, agriculture provided the South with the most readily available potential; and she was human enough to seize on it, develop herself at the expense of the Negro, fight for an institution on which depended her whole economic existence. Today, in fashion so characteristic of a closed social system, she continues to live and labor and suffer for her historic and contemporary blindness. Charles Sellers, Jr., says in his book, *The Travail of Slavery:* "Slavery simply could not be blended with Liberalism and Christianity, while Liberalism and Christianity were too deeply rooted in the Southern mind to be torn up overnight." And he declares that, according to social psychologists, such value conflicts make a society "suggestible," i.e., ready to follow the advocates of irrational and aggressive action. "Inflammatory agitation and revolutionary tactics succeeded because Southerners had finally passed beyond the point of rational self-control." At any rate, growing up comes hard, and in the case of the South social maturity has been so consistently resisted that even today Southerners do not realize the full import of their mistakes.

In 1865 the South collapsed, exhausted, pillaged, hungry, terribly in debt, a people not only forced to bear the ignominy of defeat, but to endure the brutal and stupid Reconstruction. In addition, there was the burden of providing for some 4.5 million freed Negroes. The South had had a little experience with free Negroes—in 1860 there had been a quarter of a million of them, and they were a hated and feared minority, a threat to the poor whites and a constant incitement to the otherwise docile slaves. After the war, all Negroes were free; and since the South's greatest problem was one of existence, she meant to stay alive by the only means available to her, the production of foodstuffs. She could not survive, as she soon realized, without the help of the colored man, preferably in as close a state of slavery as legally possible. The Black Codes were the result; their object was not so much an act of discrimination against the Negro, as a move to keep him in the status of laborer, since the South had need of laborers.

The Southern approach to the reality of the freed Negroes continued to be largely economic until Congress rejected the enlightened Reconstruction Plan of President Lincoln and Andrew Johnson and adopted, instead, the measures of the Northern Radicals. The Fourteenth and Fifteenth Amendments were pushed through, whites were disenfranchised, and all Negroes were given the vote. As a result, some states were actually controlled by Negro politicians, and all through the South a heavy Negro influence made itself felt. There was, of course, a terrible reaction in the mind of the Southerner. The causes of the Negro advance were quite unimportant; and, in fact, he governed more capably than could have been expected. But what was bitterly resented was that he governed at all. One must imagine an intensely proud, autonomous people, crippled by the staggering losses of war, now treated by their countrymen as a conquered nation which must pay for its opposition by a monumental price of exploitation and humiliation. Economically, Southerners were bankrupt; their land had been the war's battleground, cities were devastated and fields were idle, their manpower was decimated, their trade ruined. Their former slaves now ruled them, wore fine clothes, ate rich food, and quickly learned the condescending airs of their former masters. All factions and classes—planters, tradesmen, shippers, poor whites, discharged soldiers—came together with a unanimous and passionate conviction: White supremacy must be re-established.

Before the war, there had been little need to stress the realities of the caste system, or of the classes that followed in its wake. The stereotypes of slavery has seen to this. But now, new conditions demanded a new emphasis. For some thirty years after 1876, the position of the Southern Negro grew steadily worse. Discrimination was the hardened and universal attitude, segregation and disenfranchisement grew side by side, as practical answers to the absence of slavery. Before the war, freedmen and whites had used the same transportation, and for some time after the Reconstruction both white and colored ate at the same restaurants, attended the same theaters, and generally shared the same public facilities. Later, the weaknesses of such a system grew only too apparent to the whites, and the law was invoked to remind the Negro of his inferior position. As for the vote, Negroes were so discouraged by the success of the Democrats in 1876 that no great numbers even attempted to vote after this time, and those who did were handled in a highly effective manner, first by illegal means, later by law. Threats, violence, failure to even count Negro votes came first; in time, a skillful rewriting of state constitutions was undertaken, for Southerners were lawful people, and it was only of secondary importance that the laws were unjust.

With the majority of Southerners, segregation was a final answer to the problem of the Negro. It aimed to provide the only possible substitute for slavery, a white form of insurance for both present and future. Unfortunately, the desires of the Negro were not consulted, as somehow being marginal to the tragedy, nor was any reckoning made upon the multiple and profound influences imposed by the outside world as the years passed. The Southerner simply came to think himself invulnerable to these.

This is the Southern embarrassment, then: nourished on mother's milk; bred in family life; growing in the isolation of tradition and social custom; complicated by fierce emotionalism; confused by a philosophically and theologically barren religion; fed by hardheaded Yankee pragmatism and knowhow, and generally resting upon a foundation of fear. Fear of justice, one supposes, fear of retribution, fear of competition, fear of a hated and misused rival whose surprising strength and resiliency rests with weapons which the Southerner does not understand because he would never condescend to learn them. And finally, and most terribly, a fear that cannot be diagnosed because it involves the unknown present and the hidden future. The cry of States' Rights and the Purity of the Races are rather pitiful gestures, inept attempts by the Southern white to present to the world a front of sweet reasonableness, unrecognized by him as the ravings of a dying social order. The tenets of Christianity, the pronouncements of law, the mounting determination of the Negro, the pressure of national and world trends, these he does not understand, for his gaze is riveted upon his own immediate situation; he cannot open his eyes before the larger vision of others. The head of the Louisiana State Sovereignty Commission once made the incredible statement that the only hope for the South was to undertake the education of the whole remaining country, to convince the North that Federal insistence upon civil rights was masking an attempt to strip the states of their powers. He spoke at a White Citizens Councils' meeting, and the applause was light, for after all, he was attempting to be reasonable, and the people were suspicious of his attempt.

III

In order to grasp better the over-all scope of the race question, it seems worthwhile to consider the North and the West, for both sections share roughly the same mentality in this regard. Both sections have been widely regarded by the Negro (though less so now) as areas which will acknowledge his right to be a man. How mistaken he is, a northward or westward flight will shortly and brutally demonstrate. Nonetheless, Negroes are fleeing today in progressively greater numbers to the urban centers of the East and Midwest and to California in the West. In all these areas, they invariably meet a kind of discrimination all the more odious because of its unfamiliarity, and its unexpected character.

Why does it exist there, where one is less prepared to find it than in the South?

First, it is helpful to realize that Negroes do not qualify as members of the usual minority groups, whether they be national or religious in type. When the great waves of immigrants hit America after the Civil War, through the 1900s and into the present century, they were generally welcomed by Americans as means of populating and developing the country. Once the settling of the West became complete, however, the condition of the new national groups became harder; the land was settled, and the immigrants had little choice but to congregate in the slums of the large cities of the East and Midwest. Their situation there was close to tragic, as the history of New York's East Side can witness. But there was still much in their favor. The American theory of equality, never quite denied in the North, the gradual disappearance of the language barriers, the widely available public education, the thrift and toughness of the newcomers, the hope for a decent future which the national character subtly imparted to them, all these contributed to make the immigrant quite thoroughly American in two or three generations. So, in spite of the prejudice, in spite of the resistance given the newcomer because he was "different," in spite of the derogatory names attached to national groups, Americans are commonly persuaded that the nationals of Northern and Southern Europe, of the Near East, and even of Mexico will someday be incorporated, will become part of the fabric of American life, will be, in the fullest sense, American.

Not so with the Negro, nor with other colored peoples, notably the Chinese and Japanese. Instead of efforts to assimilate them, considerable talent and ingenuity is mustered to resist their presence, to herd them into groups and ghettos, and even to advise them to develop a racial pride of their own. In this situation, the plight of the Negro is worst of all. Unlike the Chinese and Japanese, the Negro had no national culture to fall back upon for support. He is the prisoner of the culture of the white man, who yet refuses him wholesale entrance into that culture. And supporting this consistent and widespread rejection of the Negro is a folklore so universal that it is national in scope. It is a belief that there is no worthy niche in American society for the Negro because he cannot be assimilated; that he cannot be assimilated because he is inferior, and that he is inferior because he is colored. Reductively, the badge of inferiority rests almost wholly upon skin pigmentation, which has, in the American mind, connotations of base origin, faraway sweltering lands, strange customs and superstition, and for want of a better word, downright "otherness." In a way, we are considering sort of a kind of condemnation by association; the Negro is rejected because his person is housed in dark lineaments which suggest obscurely mysterious beginnings and a local history no less odious for having been caused by the white man.

So a summary of the Negro tragedy would run something like this. The whites have faced the Negro with the pressure of white culture, have standardized the credentials for acceptance, have withdrawn the prize for want of the one badge— the white skin. Here we have the most remarkable manifestation of the extension of slavery, the "un-freedom" of not being able to reject the culture, nor to accept it. It is enough to blast the sensibilities of all but the most callous to see the Negro grope with frantic single-mindedness for all the materialistic trivia which will make him more acceptable—status-seeking, social selfishness, credit-buying, family limitation, striving to be a white man's Negro—only to be laughed at for his efforts.

But to particularize the problem more in terms of Northern outlook. Until recently, there have been other concerns in the North which kept race relations at a distance from close scrutiny. The more rapid tempo of life, the labor problems of a highly industrialized society, the articulate demands of Northern farmers, the continuous mass immigration of foreigners, and the fact that numerically the Negro formed such a slight percentage of the population, all these thrust his voice and presence into the background. This was true until very recently. Not so now. The Negro today is being pushed from the land by world competition with Southern agricultural products, by a national agricultural policy long prejudicial to his interests, by rural automation, and by his own increasing refusal to tolerate the discrimination of the South. Consequently, there exists a mass exodus to the North and to the West. The Creole Negroes of Louisiana and Texas move to California in great numbers; their darker brethren of Alabama, Mississippi, Tennessee, Kentucky, and Arkansas migrate to Detroit, Chicago, and Cleveland, while the Georgia, Florida, and Carolinas Negroes move largely to Washington, Baltimore, Philadelphia, and New York City. (Los Angeles receives 1,700 Negroes monthly; Chicago, 2,000 every month; New York City, 1,400.) It consoles the Southerner considerably that what has been a sectional question is now a national problem, and the Northerner has come to see the truth of this situation with reactions that are quite predictable. Some people in the North feel that if too much is done for the Negro, the word will spread, the colored will receive encouragement to move in, making the present burden intolerable. Others are resentful over the shouldering of an onus which has traditionally been a Southern one; they point with righteous pride to their own cities, as though a Utopia had, in fact, drawn the Negro North. Northern city officials even loudly maintain that Negroes should be educated to remain South; this with a view, of course, to have them abstain from coming North. Back and forth the buck is passed. The South is guilty, introspective, and sensitive; the North, self-righteous, hypocritical, and unwilling to involve itself in a problem which, as it declares, it fought the Civil War to solve.

The Northern position is as clearly a form of escapism as

the Southern, lacking even the merit of the profound emotion so often exhibited in the South. Northerners are avid to hear of Southern racial strife, while they tend to minimize all local news except crime. Northerners will allow the most serious breaches of justice in housing, education, and economic opportunity in their own cities, while vehemently decrying the segregation of education in the South. The North has attempted an impossible piece of indoctrination—that no problem exists; the façade erected to keep the problem out of sight has been ingenious, ruthless, and highly effective. On a large scale, the Negro simply does not exist; locally, there is an education to ignorance, furthered by a cold, dispassionate decision. Very simply, nobody wants to get involved.

So if one were to sum up the attitude of our country, he would perhaps see it as a mixture of emotional rejection and callous indifference. Indeed, we regard the Negro as some kind of mistake on the part of God. And this situation rests largely on the shameful fact that an educational offensive against racial intolerance, one going deeper than the platitudes and generalities from the Bill of Rights that Americans love to quote, has never been seriously attempted in America. The churches have made only a limited impression in this area, and our educational system, even our private schools of religious affiliation, have had only negligible success in teaching what it is to be American and Christian. Finally, the Federal government, before President Truman's integration of the Armed Forces and the Supreme Court decision of 1954, conveniently concerned itself with more important matters.

IV

Now we come to a facet of the race question which intimately concerns the Catholic: the inadequate attention given by the Church to an issue of crucial importance. Why, we might logically ask, were Catholics largely involved in forming a cooperative school system in New Orleans, in defiance of an integration order? In this same city, why were a group of Catholic laymen so little affected by the just authority of their bishop as to protest integration directly to Rome? Is it accidental that the greatest foe of integration in Louisiana, and perhaps in the South, is a Catholic, a man who has spared no effort to label integration a Communist plot? Why has no word been said of Catholic membership in the notorious and powerful White Citizens Councils? Why must, until a few recent years, Louisiana Negroes go north to attend a Catholic college, or to Texas or Alabama? Why must the participation by a priest in the sit-in demonstrations in Oklahoma City evoke such fierce controversy, or for that matter, be considered anything more than a desperately needed protest by a man whose vocation is to resist evil and injustice? Why would the demonstration movement see so little of Catholic participation, and why would Catholic membership in the civil-rights groups be so limited? Why do Catholics in the North panic as readily as their non-Catholic neighbors at the mention of a Negro in the neighborhood? Why haven't the Catholic Interracial Councils been complemented by new Catholic structures, whose intensity of training and scope of competency can deal with the mounting urgency of the problem? Why do our pulpits commonly interpret the life of a Christian as a succession of "don'ts," rather than echoing to repeated challenges and opportunities? Why is the Catholic appraisal of the injustices done the Negro the most comprehensive and the most true, and yet an academic appraisal, which too seldom issues in action? There are certainly reasons for all of this, and the reasons go deeper than references to human frailty, lack of vision, or the difficulty of reconciling principle with practical judgment and action.

For the most part, American Catholics are of European origin, and the faith that our ancestors brought to this country was characteristically European. They were still in reaction against the pressures of the Reformation, still fighting laicism and anti-clericalism, catechetics and apologetics were still defensive, the Church was still bent upon inner consolidation as a means of preserving its existence. And paradoxically enough, Catholics arrived with a superiority complex, still regarding themselves as sole possessors of truth and goodness, still sending out foreign missionaries with the conviction that European culture and catholicism were inseparable and that the interests of Church and state were often identical. These attitudes inevitably clashed with the double opprobriums facing the immigrant on these shores, that of being new ethnic arrivals and that of being Catholic. The only immediate solution for the newcomer was to dig in and hold on. And when the strangeness of the new land had disappeared, he began to fight with the weapons at hand—to learn the language if necessary, to work with all his energy and determination, win the vote and representation, go to school to compete with the natives, hope for his children, grow old and die. Priests came with the immigrants; they were pioneers like their people, often the only educated men in their communities, and for that reason, the acknowledged leaders. And so the familiar pattern of a double task appeared; to make life livable by insuring Catholic special interests, and, as an action only loosely related to the new life here, to save one's soul. The fight for survival and the otherworldly cast of mind these people had known as Europeans solidified in adapting itself to new surroundings and to a new set of social conditions. In return, the Church asked little, requesting only that her children be obedient, that they use her riches of grace, and that they support her.

So an approach to life in this country was formulated in the most practical terms. The Church was to act as sort of a social and spiritual mother, the parish would be the local refuge where the protection and consolidation of the secular and eternal orders would go on. There was no doubt in anybody's mind whom the Church favored; Catholics were her children; and favoritism had its own rewards. Catholic schools were set up, partly to capitalize on freedom of religious instruction, mostly to protect the young who would form the next generation. Church architecture was essentially European; it showed elements not only national, but period as well; Romanesque, Renaissance, Gothic, Baroque, combinations of all of these, and variations of the combinations. Mostly, Church architecture suggested a divorce from the drab, hard community existence, and a call to another world—the Church buildings were a foreign import, and after all, Heaven was a foreign country open to few without the Catholic trademark. Worship was an awesome and remote drama, the sanctuary a Holy of Holies where the priest drew the Divine Presence to the altar in a foreign tongue. The Mass was an obligation rather than an opportunity, the Sacraments defined the Catholic as good or bad, depending on the frequency of reception, for they were a means to become friendly with God and stay that way. Preaching was mostly catechetical, involving a formidable series of prohibitions, and the relationship with God was frequently portrayed as a personal affair which the Catholic promoted by adroitly avoiding the many pitfalls of life. Church vocations were to marriage or to the celibate religious life; anyone who happened to fall in between was viewed askance. In higher education, as it slowly and painfully developed, Catholics were trained to professional competence, for this was a strong mode of winning acceptance; but Catholic religious training went little beyond the intensification of the traditional mold; the role of the layman was simply obedience to his superiors. Generosity was always stressed in preaching and catechetics, and a remarkable response was evident, but it was chiefly of a material kind, or negatively, a stoic endurance of the variables of life.

The result of this was a native Catholicism quite magnificent for its cohesion, its support of Church building expansion, its steady numerical growth, and the increasing group demands that it made in community and national life. The power that flowed from this united front earned recognition and a grudging respect; the Catholic vote had to be considered; the defeat of Al Smith in 1928 was as much a tribute to Catholic unity as it was an illustration of collective religious bias. Nonetheless, Catholics were more American than it was commonly admitted; they shared the American distaste for intellectualism; they had little knowledge or appreciation of esthetics, architecture, sculpture, good music or painting. The mission of the Church was the concern of the clergy, and even with them the vision of life was severely limited; through her priests the Church set up a private concourse between God and the individual, and salvation was the logical culmination of this successful relationship.

With regard to international interests, American Catholics were as isolationist as their neighbors, and though they fought with singular dedication in the great wars of this country, their desire was as intense to finish up and get back home. In spite of the great social theologians and the writings of the modern Popes, social action was not strongly present among Catholics; as yet, they were unable to reconcile authority and freedom of action an speech. Catholic morality was competent to diagnose evils; in fact, its official moral interpretation of the structures of American life and mores has been, invariably, an admirable appraisal. But Catholics seemed incapable of providing a theological basis for a course of action; the gap between conscience and service seemed too wide —there always seemed to be more immediate problems. Moreover, Catholics knew almost nothing of the role of the layman. The Church operated on the clerical level rather than in corporate areas where the great questions of life were being forged. As a result, the momentous fights for social justice—child labor legislation, woman suffrage, labor—were won in general without a Catholic vanguard. Secular forces, other Church groups, constitutional interepretations of law—all of these educated Catholics in embarrassing fashion. And even up to the present, the blight of segregation is proving that the implications of the past are largely lost on us, since the ignoble pattern is being verified anew. Catholics are still doing little to disprove the popularly held notion that they are safe, hidebound, and conservative, illustrating admirably in their lives the great misinterpretation that "the Church moves slowly."

The history of the Negro in the American Church is quite possibly the outstanding example of our lack of social awareness. The rather considerable seepage of Negro Catholics from the Church following the Civil War was due primarily to the separation of Negroes from Catholic slaveholders, to the gross discrimination practiced in Catholic Churches, and to the active evangelism of the Baptists and Methodists. Then foreign missionaries, requested by the American bishops, came to this country to labor among the colored. The story of these men, the Mill Hill Fathers, will probably be never fully known. Their identification with the Negro and the ostracism that it implied, their dire poverty, the bitter and seemingly hopeless battles they fought for human rights, the fact that like their people they were ignored, forgotten, resisted, and silenced—all this is a chapter in Catholic history as glorious as it is obscure. In time, the American Josephite Fathers broke off from this original foundation, having attracted a few native vocations. Mother Katherine Drexel founded the Blessed Sacrament Sisters and directed their apostolate to the Negro and the American Indian. And other societies appeared on the interracial scene, notably, the Society of the Divine

Word, the Missionary Servants of the Blessed Trinity, and the Society of Jesus. But for the most part the Church pursued a parallel course with the approach of American society; no widespread or concerted efforts were made on behalf of the Negro. This fact is strikingly illustrated by the 3 percent of American Negroes who are baptized Catholics, by the tiny number of Negro priests (approximately 150), and by the refusal of many American Sisterhoods to accept Negro vocations. There are still powerful currents dedicated to perpetuating the second-class status of the Negro Catholic and the privileged status of the white Catholic. It is not to be wondered at that outspoken Negroes, who are critical of the Christian response to segregation, will list the Catholic Church (with the Episcopalian and Methodist churches usually) as a "white man's" church. Finally, we can recall as further demonstration of this point that only three Southern dioceses were integrated prior to the Supreme Court decision: St. Louis, Missouri; Washington, D.C.; and San Antonio, Texas. The first two are Northern as much as Southern, and the third possesses more of a Mexican problem than a Negro one.

Within the Church, whether North or South, the Negro is the last considered, the last listened to, the last for whom anything is done. (Though the general pattern is changing, though the most hopeful signs are evident, in terms of white debility of conscience and the frightful toll that the Negro continues to pay, the Catholic response is fearfully distant from the need.) One sees operating in this issue, at all levels of Church life, a frightful opacity of judgment and sensitivity—middle-class and white-centered mores which are singularly resistant to the reality and evidence of a full-scale social revolution. It is, indeed, matter for conjecture whether the Negro will ever take Christianity seriously after experiencing the inhumanity that Christians so capably live.

V

Perhaps our discussion clarifies the general truth that the Catholic approach to the world, or to society, or to a social disease like segregation is, in the practical order, not only wrong, but that it is wrong because it lacks a proper dynamism that will result in a powerful public impact. Our enervating "prudence" and delay loses great opportunities and serves only to perpetuate injustice. The Catholic fight for American identity, a historical course of action defensible years ago, lacks all validity and pertinence now. Yet it remains true that our ideals are not theologically sound, nor sufficiently flexible to bear complex application to the complex needs of society; they lack intensity, insistence, and practical impact. We have become a Church of administrations and institutions, expressions of our consuming desire to "belong," to win a secure niche for ourselves, and with our energies engaged in erecting and maintaining our structures we often forget why we raised them at all. The explanation for our failure cannot be sought, I would think, in our American pragmatism. I rather venture that we have imposed upon ourselves a kind of reverse secularism, an ignorance of the works that follow on viable belief, a blindness toward the connection of faith with the issues of time and society. How many Catholics, indeed, are aware that the treasures of Catholic thought must have an outlet worthy of themselves, or that the same Catholic riches are lost in huckstering and selfish trifling? How many Catholics are so acutely aware of their relationship with God as to realize that love of Him is tested by involvement with His works, and particularly His highest work, the perfection of the community of man? How many Catholics reflect that the mechanics of our worship actually orient man to the world and give him a hold upon it, and that in redeeming the world he redeems himself? The great modern Pontiffs have taught this, beginning with Leo XIII through John XXIII and our present Pope. All have stated in the most explicit terms that spiritualized social action defines the Catholic. Yet it is no exaggeration to say that we are decades behind their thought. Social research and even mere observation confirms the fact that the outstanding distinction between the Catholic and his non-Catholic neighbor is what the Catholic does on Sunday morning.

Finally, our selfish and self-condemning refusal to take up more actively the burdens of society, our Catholic retreat from the world—how dangerous and unfulfilling it is to us personally, how it compromises the Church and creates an image of her that is false, repugnant, and scandalous to men, how it paralyzes the interests of our country and hinders the ways of peace! For we show no reluctance in noising abroad the claims of the Church, we suffer no arbitration of her deposit of truth, we easily repeat the lofty message of Our Lord. But in the desperately important work on behalf of those who need us, in the hard and hot work of the vineyard where hope is extended, solidarity established, and brotherhood won—it is here that we fail or fail to be present.

For we have yet to learn that we exist for the Church as much as she exists for us. We have yet to learn that the riches of our thought are useless if they do not issue in riches of life. We have yet to learn that if we fail the poor and the social outcast they will fail us in turn by a subtle revenge, leaving us to our middle-class churnings and collective denials, leaving us to an inbreeding that will destroy us. As Dr. Samuel Miller says: "Religion justifies its existence by what it does with the world. Otherwise, it is a thing incestuous."

One conviction occurs in closing. The Negro, and others that we equate with him, will have his rights with or without us. The force of world opinion, the demands of the cold war, the preponderance of non-white peoples in the world, the increasing power of the new nations, the general population expansion, the rapid development of communications, the strong tendency toward international government, the vast inequities of wealth and poverty, power and impotence—all these create a pressure and a direction that we would be helpless to oppose, even if we wished. I do not suggest, therefore, any measure so supine and unworthy as joining a trend for fear of losing our invested interests. I suggest rather that the Church lavish upon the emerging peoples the tremendous resources of her truth and charity, save them from despair, from extreme, violent reaction, identifying their interests with her own, looking upon them as her most favored children, for so Christ would have regarded them. I suggest that the Church avoid temporizing like a plague, that she prefer fortitude to "prudence," realizing that her problem is not the acceptance of the Negro, but the acceptance by the Negro of herself. I suggest that the Church make normal and usual the convictions of a growing host of Catholic hierarchy, clergy and laity, who see the colored peoples as brothers, as new blood, as unrivaled organs of new expansion and strength. Finally, I suggest that this be done quickly, for the time is short, the issues are narrowing. The future of the Church, our country, and the world depends directly on the solution of certain key human problems, to whose presence the whole of mankind reacts today, immediately and unanimously, and with astonishing sensitivity.

7. *The Church and the World*

It is a source of immense hope today to see Christians profoundly concerned with the relationship of the Church to the world. Some will not hesitate to call this concern the beginning of a return to the world; some (Protestants among them) will see it as a break with Constantinism, or an emergence from the Counter-Reformation. Others will deal responsibly with the thesis that Christians are now involved in a new Reformation. Whatever the view, however, the current renewal aims at a realignment of Church and world; it acknowledges the existence of a new era and the socioeconomic revolution behind it; it insists that the Church has the right and the duty to speak to modern man; it admits, in turn, that man has much to say to the Church of moral, political, and social life. It is now becoming more clear that the Church, through the Vatican Council, through ecumenism, through the scriptural-liturgical resurgence, through the lay voice, is attempting to give man a more viable interpretation of the Good News of Christ, an interpretation which is historically pertinent to his condition, less intent upon institutional preservation, freer and readier to serve, older and yet ever new. To Pope John, so responsible for Christian renewal, can be attributed the same significant feat that Protestants attribute to Luther: "He enabled what had been building up to burst forth."

What does the Church have to say about life? This is the fundamental question facing us. And because the answer must be directed to contemporary human life, the Church must witness to it as it is—burdened with racial prejudice, under racial oppression, in the uncertainty of cold-war stalemate, in the Marxist grip, in the Latin American *favelas*, in malnutrition, intellectual confusion, and so on.

What is confusing us is the discovery that it is not enough to approach man continually from our end, to decide continually what is best for him from a Church standpoint, to tell him that he is not a Christian, or that he must become a Christian, or that he must subscribe to the pattern of moral and liturgical formulas that supposedly identify the Christian. More particularly, it is not enough to wave the catechism at him; nor is it enough to tell him to be good and fair, to be prudent and law-abiding, to be wary of "causes" and extremism.

It is an entirely different thing, one far more expressive of the spirit of the Gospels, to experience his life, to feel his material or spiritual poverty, to sense his bewilderment and psychological tension, to understand the reasons for his dilemma of family, human relationships, existence itself. The Church is ponderously attempting a new beginning with man; attempting to start with him in both his reality and his exigency. This was, after all, what Christ did as He opened His dialogue with the world: "He had compassion on them, because they were like sheep without a shepherd" (St. Mark 6:34).

On September 29, 1963, Pope Paul gave an inaugural allocution which opened the Second Session of the Council. It was an outstanding talk, one which was historic in openness and vision; one which put him solidly in support of the renewal begun by Pope John. This "updating" of the Church, as the Pope preferred to call it, would be attained through an investigation quite thoroughly Christological. In the course of his words, Pope Paul portrayed Our Lord with extraordinary power and precision—He is the Lord of the Church, the One

Mediator between God and man, the one source of truth, from which our thought and action must be drawn. Pope Paul sees the Church as the contemporary Christ, the Lord alive in His members, but nonetheless, a Body whose divine element is rooted in fallen humanity, which under influence of the divine, must purge itself, grow, and mature. The social movements which characterize world society are unconscious allies of the Christian aims of peace, justice, and life in Christ; so the Church must identify with these abrupt and powerful forces to give them a Christian cast and a Christian hope. "The living Church," the Pope said, "must always correspond to the living Christ."* He then outlined the four areas of concern of the Council: the Church's self-awareness, her reform, the unity of Christians, the Church's relation to the modern world.

II

In the early Christian centuries, as St. Augustine maintained in his exchange with the Donatists, a central question among the faithful was, "Which is the true Church?" During the sixteenth-century reform, the question had become, "What is the Church?" Now the current version is, "Why the Church?" Modern man has generally ceased to look to the Church for any great interest in his condition, and his skepticism rests upon the overwhelming evidence that the Church is "for" those who are "for" her—those who have the time and penchant and money to invest in her as another form of security.

Or, to investigate another reason for the modern "why"— it springs partly from the attempted dogmatic answer to the reformation question, which laid down very explicit standards for membership in the Church. This emphasis upon credentials, often bereft of any sort of living witness, surrounded the

* Pope Paul, "Inaugural Allocution," *New York Times*, Sept. 30, 1963.

Church with an aura of exclusiveness which did very little to
interest the masses or the intellectuals.

Pope Paul's first concern, therefore, is the grasp that the
Church has of herself, what the Spirit has taught her of herself, her self-awareness. More simply, this would be the meaning that she would attach individually and collectively to the
word *Christian*. From what she knows of this, and what she is
continually learning, will flow her own essential being to the
world, in thought, dialogue, and service. According to the
Pope's mind, a vital awareness of herself, and its consequent
communication to the world, will come not from dogmatic
definition of her reality, but "by faithful adherence to the
words and utterances of Christ, by respectful attention to the
teaching of ecclesiastical tradition, and by docility to the interior illumination of the Holy Ghost."* It will come from a
focus of attention upon her own mystery, which transcends
concept and terminology, and which can be clarified further
by God's revelation alone. "The Church is a mystery," the
Pope said, "a mysterious reality imbued with God's presence,
and for that reason, she is ever susceptible of a new and
deeper investigation."†

It is this "deeper investigation" upon which we are now
embarked, beginning with the prophetic initiative of Pope
John and continuing under the leadership of Pope Paul. This
"investigation" covers the whole range of conciliar interests,
but which we have seen directly as the schema on the Church.
Discussion on the schema by the Council Fathers, though still
inconclusive, began preponderately with terminology from
the Scriptures—people of God, mystical body, spouse of the
Lord—each of which transcends conceptual definition, each
of which communicates more of the hidden reality, leaving
the field open for an apprehension guided by God's Word

* Pope Paul, *op. cit.*
† Pope Paul, *ibid.*

and God's Spirit. Whatever the image used relative to the Church—single vine, single building, single temple, single kingdom, single flock—we are led to a deeper consideration of this mysterious family of God, this sign of unity with Christ, this spiritual-physical means which the Lord uses to call all men to Him.

Is the commonly superficial and unreflective grasp of the Church at the base of whatever failure we might have had with the world? The Pope says so repeatedly by implication, and the Council by its objectives. Critics—some out of love, some from other motives—have accused Catholics of a narrow and religiously jingoistic view of the Redemption, of arrogance or smug indifference toward the non-Catholic and non-Christian world, of ambiguity and immobility toward the great social crises of our times. Why should the Church, it is argued, invest more and more of her resources in an institutional framework, an inbreeding which often makes her ponderous and insensitive and even oblivious to human needs? Why would the welcome given by Pope John to non-Catholics, Jews, and Communists cause such consternation? Why should the Church leave the cold war to men like Bertrand Russell and to a tiny group of "peace" churches? Why has the Church spoken so diffusively and comprehensively on race, while seemingly incapable of effective action for the Negro? The truth of these indictments, the more numerous and painful they become, comes very close to telling us what our view of the Church is, with its vagueness, illusion, and even superstition.

Why, therefore, is there this un-Christian tendency among us to view the Church as a religious comfort station, as buildings and rules and liturgy apart from lives of men and women, as an endowment from God with no strings attached? It may be that our opacity bids us forget that the Church was built upon the cornerstone of natural human unity; that the

Church was the Redemption of Christ for the restoration of human unity. In short, that man was originally one; that he became many through sin; and that the Church was founded to remake him one through the unifying force of God's life.

If we must look to the Scriptures for perception in the Church's mystery, so also we must look to the Fathers for the original and restored oneness of humanity. De Lubac says that the Fathers saw human nature as one reality: "They seemed to witness its birth, to see it live, grow, develop as a single being."* With the advent of sin, human nature fell away from God as a single entity; with the advent of Christ, the Fathers saw the Bridegroom as having but one Bride, the whole human race. Gregory of Nyssa shied away from speaking of man in the plural, "any more than we ought to speak of three Gods." And he continued with this: "The whole of human nature from the first man to the last is but one image of Him Who is." As late as the fourteenth century, this tradition had a strong champion in John Ruysbroeck, who wrote: "The heavenly Father created all men in His own image. His image is His Son, His eternal Wisdom . . . Who was before all creation. It is in reference to this eternal image that we have all been created. It is to be found essentially and personally in all men; each one possesses it whole and entire and undivided, and all together have no more than one. In this way we are all one, intimately united in our eternal image, which is the image of God and in all of us the source of our life and of our creation."

Every rebellion against God, therefore, is a disruption of the bond with both God and man. Origen offered this explanation: "Where you have sin, there you have a multitude." "Satan has broken us up," asserted Cyril of Alexandria; while St. Augustine, in a symbolic treatment of Adam's name in terms of the Greek names for the direction of the compass,

---

* Henri de Lubac, *Catholicism* (New York: Sheed & Ward, 1958), p. 3.

wrote this: "Adam himself is therefore now spread out over the whole face of the earth. Originally one, he has fallen, and breaking up as it were, he has filled the whole earth with his pieces." The Fathers habitually dealt with sin in its ultimate essence—they saw its malice as separation from both God and man. And instead of attempting to chart the secondary effects of sin by making them synonymous with faulty operation in the individual, they insisted upon a view of sin as the source of natural disunion in people, as the cause of "natural cores of opposition." Even apart, then, from the notion of grace, sin breaks the unity of the divine image that we have in God, as it divorces us from the unified expression of this image in the race of man. In this sense, the sinner is a misanthrope; he is essentially ostracized and, as such, a threat and a parasite to the remainder of humanity. Infidelity to God does not completely destroy the natural unity of the human race—it rather makes the attainment of unity more impossible, since it immobilizes the only force that can reconcile man within nature, the Life of God. Without this Life, nature attacks itself and becomes its own greatest enemy through the unhealthy individualization of sin.

The advent of the Son of God in the world radically confronted the helpless disunity of the human race with the hope of the New Man in Christ. The action of the Word in the Incarnation meant the assumption of human nature, but also, the virtual taking of all men within Himself. St. Hilary calls the Incarnation not only a becoming of God in human nature and flesh, but an incorporation of human nature into God. Origen, in daring and mysterious language, makes this explanation: "In making a human nature, it is human nature that He united to Himself, that He enclosed in Himself, and it is the latter, whole and entire, that in some way He uses as a body." Fr. De Lubac offers a remarkable synopsis of the depth and vista of Christ's Redeeming Act in these few words:

"Whole and entire He will bear it then to Calvary, whole and entire He will raise it from the dead, whole and entire He will save it. Christ the Redeemer does not offer salvation merely to each one; He effects it, He is Himself the salvation of the whole, and for each one salvation consists in a personal ratification of his original 'belonging' to Christ, so that he be not cast out, cut off from the whole."*

The "new man" of Pauline terminology emerged from the Redemptive Sacrifice of Our Lord; the Christ that rose on Easter had reconstituted in Himself the pristine unity of the one organic nature, the one divine image that human nature was. Enmities and barriers had been broken in Him on the Cross, He Himself had become the minister of reconciliation, "has broken down the intervening wall of the enclosure, the enmity, in his flesh" (Ephesians 2:14). The Mass refers to this very reality in the Offertory: "O God, Who in a marvelous manner created human nature, and still more marvelously renewed it." When the Christian puts on the "new man" Who is Christ, having rejoined God, he has regained both the principle of his inner unity and his social unity with his neighbor. From then on, there is but the remaining obligation of realizing St. Paul's powerful admonition, "become what you are"; or in the words of St. Hippolytus: "Anxious that all should be saved, the Son of Man calls on every one of us to make up in holiness, one single perfect man." St. Maximus summarizes the whole teaching of St. Paul as to the meaning of the Christian life: "Putting on that new man, whole and entire, who was created by the Spirit in the image of God." This mystery of the new man is at once the mystery of Christ and His Church, and the development of every Christian must now be measured in his maturity against the fullness of the Whole. Christ and those who belong to Him is the new being in the world, the new creation, the master work of art of the Spirit of God.

* De Lubac, *op. cit.*, p. 9.

And it is both in God's hands and ours as to the time and dimensions of perfection that we will attain in the Spirit, and in the one Whole, Christ.

The Church, as it were, verifies these realities, since everything that is said of Christ can be said of her. She is the extension of the One Organism Who is Christ; she is the mystery of His present Being in the world. Bossuet tells us that she is "Jesus Christ spread abroad and communicated," and De Lubac clarifies this by saying, "Practically speaking, the Church is Christ for each one of us. Through her, Christ penetrates the world and everything human, aligning Himself by her sign to situations of time and human condition; He Who has finally and irrevocably triumphed as God, but Who sometimes fails in man, because man fails. The Church is the Word and Power of Christ; she is the wealth of Calvary and the Resurrection at work, and only what we have decided to be can limit what she is. She is the authority of Christ, because she has His truth, so that he who hears the Church, hears Christ and the Father Who sent Him. And it is of her constitution, explains De Lubac, that "she would also be in her members what she is for us" . . . for "each one of us, in his own small way, is the Church." Her present witness is her Lord's, a witness of hope, admonition, and service; of suffering, therapy, and peace; a witness of unity with the Father through the Holy Spirit. Through dogma, sacrament, and apostolate, she translates into human terms the great mystery of the Trinity, the reality of Persons, and the unity of nature; and she tells us, just as Christ told us, that unity is our destiny, both here and hereafter. Unity with her is more than credential or livery, it is "organic necessity," it is life. Fr. Thils comments: "It is the Church's mission to reveal to men that pristine unity that they have lost, to restore and complete it."* Natural and secular forces may work to unity, the designs of

* All the above references are from Chapter 2 of De Lubac, *Catholicism*.

God may apparently operate without her in their quiet and inscrutable way. It is no matter, all of them are to her purposes, all serve her, all are a part of the principle of unity that she is. The cohesion that she offers is the only perfect and effective one, and therefore it must be the capstone of the unfulfilled and the limited, the unity of natural man.

To bring Christians to a confrontation with the Church, so that they might know and experience her as the principle of unity—this, in turn, making them responsible for her—here we have the scope of the Council's work, which Pope John boldly called "the new Pentecost." Whatever plagues the world, whatever drives men to excesses of hate, violence, and irresponsibility, it arises from their general helplessness in face of their inner division and discord. It is to administer to this inner fractioning that Christ came, that the Church lives, that the Christian is a Christian. Let us learn what we are, and we will learn what we must do for ourselves, and for one another.

III

Given, therefore, a greater historical awareness of Christ's union with man through the Church, reform has an inevitable logic about it. The Church is the mother of life, and Christian life without reform resembles existence in a coma, or the stupor and dreams of a drug addict. Cardinal Newman understood this well, "to live is to change, and to be perfect is to have changed often."* The Church can no more deny reform than deny her life, or her mission of giving it. And if reform means relaxing the medieval and military bearing of authority, so that the hierarchy becomes more concerned with leading and serving than ruling; if it means a liturgy that ushers people into life, because it tells them in season and out what

* Cardinal Newman, *The Essential Newman* (New York: Mentor-Omega, 1963), p. 123.

witness to Christ in the community means; if it means the opening of institutions and the decentralization of Church personnel; if it means the formation and use of experimental and exploratory structures; if it means a focus upon the layman which is aware that the clergy must be the helpers of the people of God, so that they may be the Church; whatever it may mean to make men true to Christ and true to themselves, let the Church do this, confidently and unregretfully.

What we know as "church" today in Catholicism is a massive, inbred, and nearly immovable institutional structure which, without quite understanding why, possesses a mentality fairly closed, hostile to change, and nostalgic for the attitudes of conservation that came from the Counter-Reformation. By and large, the Church institutional phenomenon is more true to the nineteenth-century immigrant Church, and beyond that the Church of the Counter-Reformers, than it is to the twentieth century.

Yet it is oddly paradoxical to reflect that the Counter-Reformers (and this has some significance for the present) could draw on an immediate history of change within the Church. The medieval Church had been a reforming Church; the monastic movement was a reform movement; the mendicant orders were reforming orders; the Councils of Basle, Constance, and Fifth Lateran were meant to be councils of reform; Hus, Wycliffe, and Savonarola were understood to be signs of the need for reform; the Council of Trent promulgated its decrees *"super reformatione,"* for reforming the Church. Nevertheless, in spite of a tradition of reform attended by striking signs of its need, there was at work a powerful assumption that the best way of confronting the Protestants was not by reform, but rather by conservation, by absolutizing and institutionalizing, and by a greater reliance on precise moral and legal codes. Fr. George Tavard gives this summary of the situation so firmly entrenched even today:

"Where the Catholic mood in the Middle Ages had been one of constantly reforming the Church, trying to bring it back to its pristine purity or to bring it ahead to a restored purity, the mood of the Counter-reformation wanted to conserve not only irreformable doctrine, but also provisional, contingent, relative forms of life. The customs and laws of one age tended to be made into eternal unchanging laws."*

The profound need for the Second Vatican Council has made its point that the dominant atmosphere of the Counter-Reformation has been carried into our own century. It was and still remains an atmosphere whose theology, liturgy, structures, church government, modes of thought and be-havior are characterized by impersonality, suspicion of change, reluctance to evaluate, and an aversion to the best of the democratic process. Its tendency to preserve doctrine spread to embrace relatives which were sometimes confused with the substance of Christianity—practices and laws which often became more important than the people for whom they were made. Without lapsing into the easy judgment of hind-sight, it is safe to say that the intransigence and defensiveness of the sixteenth century has hurt the Church more than it has helped her. As a result, we have yet to understand the signifi-cant lessons of the Protestant Reform; the effects of Caesaro-Papism or identification with Western culture; or even the fact that the modern residue of this atmosphere is much more our enemy than the world.

But the vital and crucial process of reform must be has-tened. Therefore, we must familiarize ourselves with those aspects of our heritage which hinder us from response to the exigencies of the age. We must know, as Dr. Hans Kung says, "why the early Church became Jew to Jew and Gentile to Gentile, but why in later times, we have not become Arab

* Fr. George Tavard, "The Council and Reform of the Church," *Continuum*, Autumn, 1963, p. 296.

to Arab, Indian to Indian, Chinese to Chinese, Negro to Negro."* In spite of the great work done, in spite of the great outlay of human sacrifice and resource, why has our mission to these people been largely so ineffectual? The answer is complicated by historical and national nuances, but generally the fact remains: it was because our alliance was both Western and Caucasian. We have had, it is true, our De Nobilis and Riccis, our Peter Clavers and Fr. Lebbes, but the genius of these men was far too primitively Christian and far too precocious to win any widespread support from the Church of their time. Even today the Church generally refuses to make the symbolic Christian action as attitude toward world problems or non-Catholics. If a condemnation of nuclear policy were promulgated, with support of conscientious objection and non-involvement in arms industries, Western governments would react; if action on race would follow word, white support of the institutional establishment would lessen; if the poor were to be served (as seriously as the government attempts to serve them), the wealthy and middle class would be alienated. Reform, if it is to go deep enough, must reject a "theology" of the institution, even as it must reject the preferential treatment that comes from alignment with government or class.

"The first requirement of reform," says Pope Paul, "is a more diligent study and a more intensive proclamation of the Word of God."† Could it be that the Pope was implying in such a statement that our theology was incapable of being the point of departure for reform; or that it must itself undergo serious reform? It has been charged, with some truth, that Catholic theology leans toward speculation at the expense of practicality, legality rather than personalism, transcendence

* Dr. Hans Kung, *The Council, Reform and Reunion* (New York: Sheed & Ward, 1962), p. 18.
† Pope Paul, *op. cit.*

rather than immanence, institutionalism rather than corpor-
ateness, disregarding in some measure, the human, the historical, the empirical. It is quite sobering to observe, by way of
illustration, the difficulty of the Catholic in balancing Christ's
humanity with His Divinity; in seeing the historical Christ in
the Church; in recognizing the neighbor as an epiphany of
Christ. It would seem, viewing the needs of our age, that
Buber's "I-Thou" relationship would be more the concern of
our theology than the distinction between time and eternity,
infinite and the finite—or how far one may push a moral
axiom before sinning. In short, people are what matters; people are one of the two polarities in theology; people and their
organizations are the platform both for reform and mission.
And the Word of God is essential to reintroduce the Church
to people, which is about all Church reform is.

IV

It is a truism emerging from the Council that non-Catholic
reform has been largely proportionate to Catholic initiatives
in this regard. The Protestant world has well begun a vigorous reappraisal of theology, liturgy, and social witness; men
like Karl Barth, Paul Tillich, and Reinhold Niebuhr have
made an enormous impact on Western theological thought,
while Protestant scriptural work is without peer. The Orthodox have had a more difficult and more painful task in reform;
mysticism is one reason, monastic emphasis is another, so is the
tenuous position of many Orthodox under Communism.
Nonetheless, it is becoming more commonly accepted that
reform must penetrate the whole Christian church before a
common tradition can be embraced in reconciliation.

It is part of the tragedy of Christian disunion that both
Protestant and Orthodox have been caught in a historic impasse; without ceasing to think of themselves as Christian, or
as church, they have been unable to accept us as "the"

Church of Christ. We have been instead the Roman Church, the Papist Church, the Latin Church. This has been the fact, without going into the possibility of bad faith on their part or the breach of responsibility on ours. Protestants have considered us as un-Scriptural, bureaucratic, legalistic, and superstitious; the Orthodox, as overcentralized, un-Catholic in our Latinization and emphasis upon Papal precedence. But all this is changing now; the towering humanity of Pope John is still paying its dividends. We are finding that the brunt of responsibility for openness and honesty is with us; and when it is freely shouldered other Christians are quick to respond.

The Protestant reaction to what the Council has done has been invariably optimistic and grateful. Bishop Harins Lilje stated in Nuremberg at the General Synod of the United Evangelical Churches of Germany that the Second Vatican Council has forced the Lutheran Church "to rethink the question of the true Church."* He warned against suspicion of those who would be open to new beginnings within the Catholic Church: "It is impossible that a Vatican Council which has been convened against a modern background will not raise again for the whole of Christianity the question, which is the true Church and to what extent can we claim to be a church according to this creed?"† Professor D. Sucker, in a lecture given in Hamburg on the Evangelical-Catholic relationship, was even more emphatic: "Protestantism today finds itself in a tragic situation. It is maintaining a protest that has basically lost its object. It no longer confronts the Catholic Church at the point at which Luther had reason to attack it. Luther would not turn himself against the Catholic Church as he did in his own time."** Pastor Helmut Hochstetter continues in the same vein in the German periodical *Evangelische Jahres-*

* News Service of the League for Evangelical-Catholic Reunion.
† *Ibid.*
** *Ibid.*

briefe: "The courage with which the Roman Church criticizes itself calls us also to such an attitude of self-criticism. Especially helpful in achieving this is the frank and cooperative treatment of the non-Catholic observers. Church history took a turn which was not expected, although hoped for by many people. Many things will change, not only within the Catholic Church, but among us. But there will also grow many things which have languished—the love of the brethren and the strong faith that God will lead His Church through all the entanglements of men." Dr. Geoffrey Fisher's proposal for the dissolution of the World Council of Churches, so that the resulting inter-church organization would be acceptable to the Catholic Church, is another powerful sign of good faith. So is the general Protestant response to the Pope's proposal for a Pan-Christian Council over which he himself would preside.

Perhaps the most amazing example of Protestant reform has appeared from the work of Pastor Max Lackmann, the founder of the League for Evangelical-Catholic reunion in Germany. Deposed from the Evangelical Church because of his "Catholic tendencies," Lackmann founded the league for purposes of reunion. The Declaration of Principles propounded by him for the league are substantially recorded:

> The League confesses and witnesses that Our Lord Jesus has founded only one Church, which exists in the realm of the visible and is always present, and that according to Sacred Scripture and universal Christian belief, visible unity is inherent in the nature of the true Church. The league therefore deems the present division of Christians, especially the schism of Western Christianity between Catholic and Evangelical Christians as being against the will of Christ; that is to say, it is a sin and a scandal. The league bears witness that the way to unity is prescribed by Sacred

Scripture ... [which] teaches as necessary for salvation the union of an ever-acting God and man's cooperation, of Word and Sacrament, of Faith and the Law, of Office and Community. The league rejects every way to unity which contradicts Sacred Scripture or diminishes the full content of its truth. The League does not promote individual conversions, but considers corporate reunion demanded. It [the league] sees in a corporate reunion of Evangelical Christians with the Catholic Church the way which is commanded by God, the Lord of History, to the reunion of divided Christendom. The aim of corporate membership in the Catholic Church can only be achieved by furthering Evangelical Christendom's development into a churchly body. This development must fail, however, if it doesn't have corporative membership as its aim. It can only succeed if a Protestantism (of both Lutheran and Reformed stamp) is overcome. The league does not strive to blur or level off confessional differences that exist within the Evangelical Church. It is convinced that these contrasts can be overcome only if it should first enter Catholic unity. Lutherans, Reformed and United Church members who belong to the league should remain members of their religious community and should gather together Christians of their communities for the purpose of furthering corporate reunion. . . .*

The thirst of Lackmann and his followers for unity within the Church can be illustrated by portions of his book, *Credo Ecclesiam Catholicam*, which he wrote on the event of his desposition from his own communion. The evident emotion which appears in many places suggests the hurt he felt at the treatment given him by the Evangelical Church, but even more, his honest belief in the necessity of reunion. He maintains that official Protestantism can no longer be a "bulwark

* Max Lackmann, *Credo Ecclesiam Catholicam*.

of God" whose fidelity to His Will arose from its love of the Word and its profession of Truth. No longer does Protestantism lead to the one Church as the source of Divine Truth and Life—it rather leads away from the Church, and abandons the evangelical "patrimony" to ruin and destruction. He warns Christians against having anything to do with this type of Protestantism, calling it a sin against unbelievers and against a world which must be called to faith in Christ. Therefore, Protestants must have the courage to recognize their untenable position, acting not to reform Protestantism, but to transcend it. It is only in this way, he concludes, that the original goal of the Reformation can be achieved, since the Fathers of the Reformation arose within the Catholic Church to insist upon its evangelical character, and were preserved by God to make that character a reality.

Obviously, Lackmann knew his ground well in expressing sentiments like the above, knew his own position and knew the direction that the Church was taking. Men like Lackmann had not been disappointed in Pope John, nor were they to be disappointed in Pope Paul. In the same inaugural, the Pope addressed the observers (including Lackmann), and said this: "Our voice trembles and our heart beats the faster both because of the inexpressible consolation and fair hope that their presence stirs up within us, as well as because of the deep sadness we feel at their prolonged separation. . . . If we are in any way to blame for that separation, we humbly beg God's forgiveness and ask pardon too, of our brethren who feel themselves injured by us."* The reaction to the Pope's plea for forgiveness was immediate on the part of the Protestants. Dr. Hans Asmussen, himself an observer and the author of an impressive pre-Council book, wrote an open letter to the Lutheran Bishop of Munich in which he asked for "an answer to the plea for forgiveness by the Pope, for a re-examination

* Pope Paul, *op. cit.*

of the question of truth under the aspect of the gratifyingly clear Christ-centeredness of Pope Paul, and for an exhortation to laity and pastors to a new encounter with the Catholic Church."

And yet, "perfect reconciliation," according to the Pope, "was not the object now." This "blessed hour" must be awaited with patience, while every effort was spent to make it real. What we should have in common now, said Pope Paul, was "true brotherly peace." Very obviously, the type of ecumenism that is his concern has little to do with defensive polemics, or steps to convince non-Catholics of their wrong and our right, or negotiations with this or that confession about a return to the Church. Its aims are rather broader, but fully as concrete; a mutual renewal which looks to the removal of barriers, a progressively confident dialogue, the investigation of ways to collaborate in the temporal order.

The reform that aims at the unity of Christians will strip us of many things falsely identified with the absolutes of our religion. The Pope faces this possibility with calmness and objectivity: "The reform at which the Council aims is not, therefore, a turning upside down of the Church's present way of life or a breaking with what is essential and worthy of veneration in her tradition; but it is rather an honoring of tradition by stripping it of what is unworthy or defective so that it may be rendered firm and fruitful."* Whatever there is about us that is more Roman than Catholic; more Western than Eastern; more traditional than evangelical; more bureaucratic than free; more docile than courageous—all these must be put to the test of the Gospels and of human need. Otherwise, we assure the shameful continuance of religious disunity, and in the process, make irremediable the moral and social sickness of our times and our world.

* Pope Paul, *op. cit.*

V

The ultimate meaning of the Council is at once the final cause and mission of the Church, the reconciliation of the world to herself through service. The two poles, herself and the world, are fast becoming more difficult to reconcile. Christians, and particularly Catholics, are finding themselves both in a diaspora and a minority status; Latin America, where the Church claims one-third of her membership, is in a critical phase of its history, and could be either saved or lost; the Moslem, Hindu, and Buddhist worlds are for the most part unpenetrated; the issues of poverty, peace, and race deserve more decided attention; no détente with Communism is imminent, despite the bold vision of *Pacem in Terris*.

To say that the Church is in the world but not of the world is to give no practical answer at all; it fails to explain how the redemptive process engages all the structures of life, it fails to account for the stewardship of the Christian, it fails to portray the world as a home whose ungodly tendencies now must be subdued, whose evolving future now must be earned, whose eternal fullness in Christ now must be secured. "Today," wrote Pope John, "the Church is confronted with the immense task of giving a human and Christian note to modern civilization, a note that is required and is almost asked for by that civilization itself for its further development and even for its continued existence.*

It is not too much to say that the world was made for the Church, and that the Church was founded for the world. Without the world, the Church would no *raison d'être*, no membership nor raw material, no imaginable reality or purpose. Moreover, the world is of the Church; it takes its hope and direction and finality from the Church, and without her, there is no source of these. As Leslie Dewart so pertinently

* Pope John, *Mater et Magistra*.

comments: "We do not happen to exist in the world, as if we might have existed elsewhere, but the lot fell to the world. To us the world may be distant, but it can never be an alien domain. It is not a foreign land—it is our home. The reason is simple: the world in which the Church exists is the only real, human, earthly world that exists—there is no other. It is this world, therefore, the real one, that is our inheritance to be gained, our prize to be earned or, better, our charge to tend and care for. It matters little that the world does not always know this—or knows it and admits it not."*

In the unspoken presumption of Christians today that they are not of the world, nor responsible to the world, we see the common development of values that are extremely worldly, in the pejorative sense. According to this mentality, the world is understood as a place to live in, to enjoy, to use, and even to exploit; but not to direct, to endow with the stamp of one's spirit and hands, to work and suffer for. There is little sympathy for a love of the world as God loved it; little thought of redemption, as Christ redeemed it; or reconciliation, as the Spirit reconciles. The thought of the world is often a Manichean one of blacks and whites, whose devil is personified in the liberal who is "selling us out"; in the Communist, in the Negro, and the poor man; and whose god is their dollars, property, power, and ultimately, their simpleminded ease. Two moral worlds become visible: one a formula to keep God friendly, mollified, and excluded from interference with one's life; the other, a design to come to terms with society, to master its rules, to accommodate, to make concessions, to avoid insecurity of idea, act or position. Such a schizophrenic code is at the heart of the religious-secular distinction, since religion is seldom appealed to in political questions, social and economic issues, unless one's nest is threatened by progres-

* Leslie Dewart, "Christians and Marxians in Dialogue," *Continuum*, Summer, 1963, p. 142.

sives, agitators, pinks, or agents of the international Jewish conspiracy. It is not to be wondered at that Christians of this type, who purport to be unworldly, are in reality very "worldly" in their social morality, and quite indistinguishable in the rank masses of pagans that surround them.

Nor is it particularly intelligent or honest on our part to say, as we commonly do, that society is "secularistic" for having slammed its doors on religious values. It is more true to say that society could not be otherwise because of our default; we have seldom risked the expense of witnessing to something better.

It is a fact for chagrin that Christians are commonly satisfied with a religion centered about the negative, about prohibitions that clearly define unlawful action, while stating very little what one must do as Christian duty. Community attitudes, in such a climate, come off second best; the task of creating more habitable living conditions, of strengthening institutional life or creating *ad hoc* institutions, of improving human relationships through economic opportunity and better law—such imperatives are often left to the politicians, or to un-Christian humanists. The decalogue can say, "Do not steal, and you are obligated to respect the property of others," but such a precept leaves many a loophole for avoiding the positive duty of using wealth to eliminate poverty by a better distribution of goods, by creating decent jobs and the training to hold them, by regarding automation as a community concern, by guaranteeing the rights of the poor through social and legal institutions. Since we do not work to eliminate conditions which degrade human dignity, thereby making human fulfillment and salvation next to impossible, we become partners to the crime, and the human misery that we allow to descend upon others punishes us in a strict spiritual counterpart.

Let us remember that the worth of the Christian to the

world lies with the fact that he is not established; he is not tied down to a certain time, culture, or set of interests. His Christianity is timely because it transcends anything that will detract from its universal humanity. Through it, his sense of the world is so interpenetrated with his sense of God that he is able to offer the world what Henri Bergson called a "supplement of soul"—an awareness of its deeper reality, its present, and its purpose.

If our Christian "credo" possesses the worth that we claim for it, it is worth questioning, and in its present state, it is worth reform. It is worth questioning in its absolutes, as being liable to further development and more clarified expression. It is worth questioning in its relative forms, as to whether they best elucidate immutable and transcendent truth. And the instruments of test are the Gospel, the living tradition of the Church, the Holy Spirit, and the needs of men. The Church endows us with all her resources purely for engagement with life, which in the Christian sense, means other men.

Finally, the problem of the Church's face to the world is the problem of exploring love on all levels and in all its facets. Pope Paul notes that love is the "genius of the apostolate." And he continues: "We will love our brothers, whether they be close or distant. We will love our own fatherland, and will love other fatherlands. We will love our friends, and we will love our enemies. We will love all social classes, but particularly those which have most need of help, of assistance, of betterment. We will love the very young and the very old, the poor and the sick . . . We will love our time, our community, our technical skills, our art, our sport, our world."*

* Pope Paul, *op. cit.*